PASSION *for* SPORTS

PASSION *for* SPORTS

Athletes tell their stories of why they love their games

Contents

Introduction 7

Chapter 1: As a Child 9

Chapter 2: Introductions 49

Chapter 3: Senses...65

Chapter 4: Camaraderie.............................101

Chapter 5: Competition 123

Chapter 6: Adulation 153

Chapter 7: Something to Prove....................167

Chapter 8: Success 183

Chapter 9: Eyes for Another 199

Chapter 10: Does It Matter 213

Chapter 11: Hall of Fame 225

Acknowledgements

So much in sports today centers around controversies and unseemly behavior, high prices and high salaries. There is a lot to not like about sports. Among all the negative, some times you need to remind yourself that there is good that comes associated with sports.

Mike Kilduff, a senior editor with The Sporting News, had that vision. He kept that as an ideal and early in 2001, he set out to interview and coordinate a project that reminded the magazine's readers that there is good in the sports world. Specifically, he set out to rekindle the passion for sports by linking fans with the athletes, letting athletes tell why they love the games they play and, in essence, why readers should still love those games.

With a lot of assistance, from Tom Dienhart, Lee Spencer, Larry Wigge, Mike DeCourcy, Sean Deveney, Steve Greenberg, Matt Crossman, Jeff D'Alessio, Steve Walentik, Dan Graf, Stan McNeal, Kyle Veltrop, Ken Rosenthal, Rich Cimini, Mike Preston, Chick Ludwig, Nick Canepa, Clare Farnsworth, Kent Somers, Jean-Jacques Taylor, Mike DiGiovanna, Michael Silverman, Dennis Brackin, Tom Maloney, Chris Anderson, Scot Gregor, Susan Slusser, Mark Schmetzer, Chris Edwards, Michael Hunt, Lacy J. Banks, Paul Woody, Reid Creager, Charles Odum, John Delong, Ken Sins, Bob Young and Mark Montieth, Mike organized the interviews into a story that appeared in The Sporting News on August 27, 2001.

With similar passion, Mike realized he had so much material to draw upon, he wanted to package it in a book.

With more able assistance, from Christen Sager, David Walton and Bob Parajon, you're now holding the product of Mike's vision, his passion and his zeal.

When all of those headlines start to drag you down and lessen your love for the game, I hope you pick up this collection of interviews and it reminds you why you should still love sports.

Steve Meyerhoff
Editorial Director, Books/The Sporting News

Introduction

It's as if the fullback is reclining on a couch in our office, sitting like Tony Soprano across from Dr. Melfi or talking like a faceless caller to Frasier Crane's radio show.

He talks. We listen.

"I'm from Mechanicsburg, Pennsylvania, so as soon as I was able to focus my eyes, I was kind of indoctrinated into the football way of life," the fullback says. He talks more. We listen more, take some notes and make professional, encouraging remarks: *Uh-huh, and how did this make you feel?*

"You know the high school football team, those guys were gods to me. All I wanted to do was play for Cumberland Valley High School when I grew up," the fullback says.

Oh?

"Every recess, all the little kids would be out there playing football. As soon as school was over, all the little kids would be out there in the field or in someone's yard playing football." *OK, we should talk more about this. What do you remember about those times?*

"I always wanted to play in a league, but ... my parents ... I wasn't allowed to play until I was in middle school, which was such torture. They made me play soccer until then, and wrestling and swimming and basketball—everything except football. But of course I got a healthy dose of football at recess and every day after school."

We're having a breakthrough here. What you're telling us is that you really love playing this game of football. That's passion, and that's pretty powerful stuff. How does this make you feel?

"What makes a player great," the fullback says, "is his passion for the game." The fullback is Jon Ritchie of the Raiders, and football is the air that fills his lungs. He certainly is not unique, and the game of football is not exclusive. So many other individuals could slide onto our fictional therapist's couch and similar emotions would gush out.

When they do this, we, the fans, tingle.

The Sporting News talked to about 125 athletes, coaches and legends about their love for their game—its genesis, its evolution, its peak and its enduring power. In some ways, this is a love letter to sports—an emotional outpouring about all they adore in their game. This is their platform, the mike is on, the curtain is raised, and we are their audience. Here are their words with no writer to interpret or paint an image—just the thoughts of each person about his love for his game, as if he were talking about a precious moment with his own children.

Think of it as group therapy—good for them and good for us, too. They need to tell us it's not just about the money. We desperately want to believe that in the games we follow religiously, the hearts of those acting in these dramas pulse with a passion equal to our own. We are comforted by the words of baseball Hall of Famer George Brett, who says, "When I found out I could get paid (to play baseball), I thought, 'Well, that's stupid, because I should be paying them.'"

That's exactly what we thought after we first felt the magnetic tug of a sport on our souls. Over time, that feeling grows in the heart and engulfs the mind. When we love something, we can't get enough of it. This eternal flame is kindled early in life, and as Brett says, "I'm 48 years old now, but I still have a burning desire to go out there and play." The last thing Brett did as a player on a baseball diamond was kiss home plate, like a daddy leaning into the crib to place a good-night peck on his toddler's cheek or a priest bowing at the altar to close Sunday Mass. That cherished white pentagon was to Brett for so many years his baby and his pulpit. "Yeah," he says, "I guess you could say I'm passionate about it and will be until I die."

Those goose bumps remind us we know what he means.

— Mike Kilduff

CHAPTER 1

As a Child

As a Child

_____

Some say sports are childish. Others say that professional sports would be better if they were more childish.

In those formative youth years, skills were developed, teamwork was discovered and winning and losing was something you had to deal with, whether it was on the sandlot, in a pickup game or in an organized league.

Who among us wouldn't want to go back to our youth, grab a basketball and head to the local playground to see who wants to play? Or to round up some buddies for nine innings on the ballfield?

For athletes today, this is where it all began, where their passion for the game was first kindled.

As a Child

———————

Indianapolis Colts quarterback Peyton Manning

"I've always had a passion for the game, and the game has changed at every level from high school to college to the NFL, but I still have the same passion and I still get excited for games today, just like I did when I was playing in junior high. There's something about when you wake up in the morning knowing you have a game that day.

"With (my brother) Eli we had to wait until he got to a certain age before he could start playing with us. He was too small before that. It was always fun for myself and my two brothers, Cooper and Eli, to go out and play catch with my dad. That was always a great feeling to just be able to play pitch-and-catch with your dad. It's something that so many people can relate to playing catch out in the backyard with your dad.

"With Eli, I used to dress Eli up, I guess when I got to high school he was five years younger, so I had a pretty strong arm and I wanted to (play catch with him). He could throw the ball fine, but it was kind of hard for him to catch some of my passes because they were coming a lot harder, so I used to put pillows all inside his shirt and inside his sleeve to help with the padding so the ball wouldn't hurt him so much, just so he could catch the ball and get it back to me. It's kind of funny now because he's going to be the starting quarterback at Ole Miss and he's the kid I used to dress up in pillows just so he could catch my passes.

"Probably the best year I ever had playing football was my sophomore year in high school with my older brother, Cooper, who was my wide receiver. I think I completed about 130 passes that year, and I threw 80 of them to my brother. That was just a great feeling because Cooper and I grew up playing football in the back yard and to be able to do it on the football field where it really counted was a great feeling. We had our own signals, you know, he and I would draw plays up in the dirt."

Former Minnesota Twins coach and baseball player Paul Molitor

"I love this game for a lot of reasons. It's been a huge part of my life since I was 4 or 5 years old. I was drawn to the sport by a connection to watching Minnesota Twins games on television and laying in my bed at night listening to the radio broadcasts. Having been to the stadium an average of once per season for my birthday with my dad, I could picture the games from the radio broadcasts, and imagine what it was like to sit back there in left field in the second deck. When they'd call a home run for Harmon Killebrew, I could see those fans getting up and anticipating the ball heading their direction. Walking into the stadium as a kid and just the energy and the excitement and the anticipation, it really caught me, and that's how I fell in love with the game.

"Growing up in Minnesota, I spent most of my time after Christmas measuring the snow outside to see when the grass was going to appear so I could drag my dad into the backyard and he could throw the ball just high enough above the fence so I'd have to try to leap and make a home run-saving catch.

"I still remember getting involved as a youngster and playing youth baseball and the excitement of being able to wear my grade-school uniform to school after lunch because we would go straight to the game. I felt so cool because I had my uniform on sitting in classroom, especially when I was in sixth grade because I was the only sixth-grader on the team."

Former Nebraska quarterback Eric Crouch

"Ever since I was 8 years old, when I started playing football, basketball was my first sport. Running has always been a thing for me, which is why I've developed into a running quarterback.

"John Elway was my idol since I started watching football. I was glued to the TV every time they (the Broncos) were on. I wasn't a Chiefs fan. I went to Kansas City a couple times to watch the Broncos play the Chiefs. I collected football cards. I had all the sets. It was a serious thing.

"And I was the guy who always rounded everybody up in the neighborhood and said 'All right, we're playing football. I don't care if it's 90 degrees or minus-20. We're going to get the snow football game going.' ...

"I had a passion when I was 8. I had dreams of being an NFL quarterback. I don't know if that will ever happen, but it's still a dream. I'm still on the ladder to getting there. I played football because I was good at it and it was fun. I got serious when I was a sophomore. My coach built my confidence and I started getting letters from colleges. I got a letter from Nebraska. After getting that and being from here (Omaha, Neb.), that set the stage for me thinking I could become a college football player. If a program like Nebraska was checking me out and willing to offer a scholarship, then I could potentially be up there with the big guys and compete."

Oakland Raiders fullback Jon Ritchie

"I'm from Mechnicsburg, Pennsylvania. So as soon as I was able to focus my eyes, I was sort of indoctrinated into the football way of life. The high school football team ... those guys were gods to me. All I wanted to do was play for Cumberland Valley High School when I grew up. So every recess all the little kids would be out there playing football. As soon as school was over all the little kids would be out there in the field or in someone's yard playing football. So I realized it was something special as soon as I could run and as soon as I could hold a football in my hand. That's all we really wanted to do.

"I always wanted to play in a league, but ... my parents ... I wasn't allowed to play until I was in middle school, which was such torture. They made me play soccer until then, and wrestling and swimming and basketball everything except football, but of course I got a healthy dose of football at recess and everyday after school."

NASCAR driver Terry Labonte

"I've been doing this for a long time and I can remember racing quarter midgets when I was gosh, maybe 7 years old and that was like fun. We didn't get to race them every weekend, because they didn't have a track in the town we lived in. So when I started racing stock cars at about 19, I was racing against people who were actually making a living doing it. And I thought, man, that would be so cool to do that—just to be able to go out and race. I loved doing it. The last year I was in Texas I was racing two nights a week and knew that was exactly what I wanted to do. Every weekend I couldn't wait. I didn't have a job, I would work on the car all week and we'd go race on the weekend. Still lived at home with my mom and dad—didn't cost me much to live—and I still had their credit card for gas and I could get a tank a week. I thought I had it made. That was probably about the time I knew I wanted to race."

Oakland Raiders team executive and Pro Football Hall of Famer Jim Otto

"When I was a little boy I wanted to play football more than anything else. I was 11 years old when I told my grandfather, I says, 'Grandpa, some day I'm going to play for the Packers.' I grew up in Wisconsin, that's why I said that. It was in my mind, it was a goal of mine to be a professional football player at any cost."

Wisconsin basketball forward Charlie Wills

"I first knew that I loved college basketball when I was in high school on a visit to the University of Wisconsin. I was watching the Minnesota vs. Wisconsin game, a game that I will never forget. Wisconsin, the underdog, needed a victory against second-ranked Minnesota to receive a bid to get to the NCAA Tournament. The air of excitement and fever created by everyone in the gym showed me what it is to love the game of college basketball.

"I love college basketball because I can make a difference in a little kid's life. I can give him or her the confidence to believe in themselves by just spending a few minutes of my life and time with them."

Minnesota Twins bullpen coach Rick Stelmaszek

"I'm from Chicago, and the first attraction was going to White Sox games with my father and uncle. I was a Yankee fan, because of the fact that my father played in the minor league system for 10 years for the Yankees. He played with Ralph Houk, and I got to meet him and some of the players and that type of stuff. And then sitting in right field in old Comiskey Park, by the scoreboard with a cross breeze and watching a doubleheader on Sunday. ... I thought that was the neatest thing in the world. As you got close to the ballpark and saw the players, they looked like giants."

San Diego Chargers quarterback Doug Flutie

"Probably when I was 7 years old, playing flag football and going out in the backyard with my brothers, running and catching. I was never a big hitter. I played defense throughout high school, but I'd try to strip people instead of hitting them. ... I wasn't big on the collision thing."

Former NBA player Mario Elie

"It started for me just growing up in New York City. That's what the city is known for; basketball is No. 1 in New York. The courts are full all day, and you know once you lose you're done for the day.

"So guys are going hard because you don't want to lose the court and go home. So I made sure I had a good five from my neighborhood, and we'd try to stay on it all day. We used to stay on the court from 10 to 4, running all day. Sentry Park, Riverside, all the parks in my neighborhood, and all the parks in the other neighborhoods. That's where I got the fire, the hunger and the love for the game.

"It was probably 10th grade when I really, really got into it. I grew a couple of inches that summer, and a lot of guys used to watch me play in the park and a friend of mine got me into an organization so I could play in tournaments. That got me free T-shirts, trophies, sneakers. I thought, 'Hey, this isn't bad for a young guy.' Getting to play and get free stuff, a bag or something, back then that was big.

"First, I loved just playing. But second, I loved the competition. In high school in New York, it was so competitive. You're playing against the best in that city, and that's why you play the game: to be the best you can be. You play against the best competition and hold your own, then you build a reputation.

"If you had a good summer, people knew about you. My nickname was the Jedi Knight when I was growing up. I was flying around, dunking. They had guys on a microphone commentating the game, 'Here comes the Jedi!' They'd be making jokes, playing music. It was great.

"It's a reputation thing in New York. Guys know who you are even before you step in the gym, and that was a great feeling. I fell in love with it all.

"I remember walking my dog in the snow, I'd take my ball and wear my gloves so I could brush the snow off the ground, tie my dog up and just play by myself. I wasn't blessed with warm weather like somebody in California. … I'd just take my dog for a walk in the morning, brush the snow off and just shoot, work on my game, just to try and stay sharp.

"I loved those parks. I still think about it all the time. The rims got no nets. You're playing on concrete and the fence is right there. You could have major surgery if you miss a layup and somebody hits you, with a pole right under the basket. But you never thought about that stuff.

"You just played hard, knowing you could break an arm or tear a knee. But if there was no blood, there was no foul growing up in New York.

"Me and my buddies, when I go back to New York, we still go to the park and sit and watch the young guys play. I can remember thousands of people coming to watch us play. The park would be just packed to watch those games in the summer league. They loved the dunks, the amazing dribbling skills. You had guys who were great jumpers, great ballhandlers, shotblockers.

"I still get wired up thinking about it."

Charlotte Hornets forward P.J. Brown

"The reason I played this game was because my anatomy wouldn't let me go to football. My body was a basketball body from the start. I loved all sports as a kid, and it didn't matter what I was playing, I loved to win and I hated to lose. I remember being an 8-year-old kid out playing football in the cold, obviously no money involved, and I just hated to lose. At an early age I remember saying some words that I wasn't taught to say after I'd lose. Defeat has just been something that I've always had a hard time dealing with, no matter what sport or at what level."

Arizona Cardinals quarterback Jake Plummer

"I loved it from the get-go: fifth grade, tackle football at recess. You go from level to level and each one has its own benefits and negatives. High-school ball, you have all your best friends, it's Friday night. That was great. You go to college and it's even better. You get to the pros and now you realize you're at the top of the game. Some people change and (start to) think it's a job. That's the wrong way to take it. You have to remember it's a game you love to play."

Tulane basketball coach Shawn Finney

"My parents say I could dribble before I could walk. I don't know if that's really true, but I was dribbling a ball around the house since I was 1 or 2. … When I was a junior in high school, I was out mowing the grass and the lawn mower blade broke off and hit my leg. I went running over to my house and my father comes out and my mom's in a little bit of a panic. They scoop me up and I'm in the car flying to the hospital and all I'm saying is, 'I'm not going to get to play basketball. I'm not going to get to play basketball.' My mom says, 'You'll get to play basketball. You'll get to play basketball.' And I tell her, 'Yeah, but not tonight.'"

Former Oklahoma linebacker Rocky Calmus

"I realized (I liked playing football) in third grade. I liked it so much I didn't want to play flag football, I wanted to play tackle football. But they didn't have it for third grade, but they had it for fifth grade. … My first big contact was during a game across the street from our house. I was playing with my brothers and his older friends. The biggest guy, he seemed like a lineman now. I just went up and hit him. He knocked me really hard, but I tackled him. I'll never forget that."

NFL defensive back Blaine Bishop

"Probably in junior high, that's when I realized that this is something that I'm special at because at that time I keep hearing people telling me and then I finally realize that things are coming so easy for me. I played other sports, but football was the one that I excelled at."

Connecticut basketball coach Jim Calhoun

"I always had passion for baseball and football in high school. Then, when my dad had died, and I left school for about a year plus to work, I missed school some, I missed my friends some, but I really missed playing. I couldn't wait to get back to school, and when I got back, I had a lot of success. My team went to the Division II semifinal, and all those good things happened. I just realized that, and for the same reason I started coaching. I tried out with the Celtics, got cut and was deciding what to do, and my coaches convinced me to come back, maybe start working on a master's degree, and they put a whistle around my neck and walked out on the court, and I said, 'This is it. This is what I could do.'"

Indiana Pacers guard/forward Ron Artest

"Basketball just sort of grew on me when I was a kid, just being so competitive. I stumbled into the game and just happened to be very athletic and loved to play games like tag and stuff. I could run faster than the other kids and nobody could catch me. I was also tall, and that helped. I was also a pitcher in baseball and a quarterback in football. But I turned out to be a better player in basketball."

Colorado quarterback Craig Ochs

"The first CU game I went to was in 1986, when they beat

Nebraska for the first time in 20 years or so. That's my first memory of Folsom Field. I was 5 at the time. Since then, it evolved into a passion. I probably didn't miss a CU game in the 1990s. I've always loved football. When I was younger, I was a big kid and it was the only sport I could play for a while. I had Eric Bieniemy's jersey and hat. I have a lot of funny pictures of me dressed in a Colorado uniform.

"I used to get really nervous before games. We went to the 1991 Orange Bowl, when we beat Notre Dame (to win a share of the national title). By the third period, I had to go to the bathroom. During that time, Bieniemy scored the only touchdown of the game. Of course, I missed it. But I've seen the replay about a thousand times. I still get nervous before a game."

New Jersey Nets coach and former NBA player Byron Scott

"I knew I loved the game when I was 14, but ironically I played baseball and football until I was a junior in high school. It wasn't until I was 17 that I decided basketball was the sport for me. Baseball, to me, if I wasn't pitching or getting a ball hit to me at shortstop, was boring. Football has so much contact that I knew I wouldn't be able to do it for that long. With basketball, there was always something happening, and being a kid, I enjoyed that type of atmosphere. You never get bored."

Mississippi quarterback Eli Manning

"My passion for the game started when I was with my brothers. They are 5 and 7 years older, and I looked up to them. Being able to go out in the front yard and throw with them always was a thrill for me. Being included with their friends in the front yard. It really took off when I began playing flag football in fifth grade. Me and my buddies took it to the extremes where we had our own signals and checks at the line. It was fun being out there throwing touchdowns, putting in new signals, putting in trick plays. I remember a few of my checks. It wasn't too complicated. It was a color or a number. We still talk about it."

Big Ten commissioner and former college basketball player Jim Delany

"My brother and his friends played in the backyard and as a little kid, you couldn't get in the game. When you did, it was a thrill. Notwithstanding that the basket was probably 9 feet and there were gravel pits underneath it where people regularly sprained their ankles. You didn't really draw a charge, but you did run into the garage door on any drive. And all of the windows were broken out. You can imagine that in a working-class neighborhood. Every day, everybody was there, just waiting for a game."

Chicago Bulls guard/forward Jalen Rose

"When they first started playing games on CBS, I was watching the games. After the game went off I used to go outside and emulate the moves. My friends and I built a full court. We put two milk crates on top of each other, got two long poles from the lumber yard and a square piece of wood and made a full court in the alley. … We used to play all the time under the street lights, 24/7, against other blocks. It was non-stop competition."

Former LSU linebacker Trev Faulk

"I was about 8 or 9 when I became passionate about the sport. Me and a friend played on a dead-end street by his house every day. Then we played in middle school and high school. Now, we both play in college. We enjoyed the competition the most."

Los Angeles Lakers guard Kobe Bryant

"I have been loving basketball since I was a little kid playing with my dad. I'm a little different because I grew up with it, with my dad. As I continued to grow, it just became such a part of my life, and my love for it just got greater and greater every year.

"I still love to play; I just love the game. It's something you can play when you're mad or upset. Even now I will go and I will just shoot and take my mind off things. When I was younger, if I was mad at my parents because they would not let me go out or I was in trouble for something, that's what I would do. Pick up a basketball and go shoot. They could not stop me from doing that. It's a little bit of escapism. If you go and you have a ball and a rim, you take yourself somewhere else, in your mind at least.

"I think our game has a very wide-ranging appeal because of that. Everybody loves playing this game, even if you can't play a lick. You like going out there and throwing the ball up, and just seeing if it goes in. That's basically what we do, we just make it more complicated. But anybody can shoot a basketball, you don't have to be one of us. It's an enjoyable game, one everyone can relate to."

Former President and Michigan offensive lineman Gerald Ford

"As a young lad, we had a playground right near my house, and I kind of fell into playing regular sandlot football. Truth was it wasn't a grass park. It was dirt and gravel. In those days it wasn't organized like it is today. And when I played in high school, I loved the competition. I was successful in high school. I played three years on the high school football team. I was all-city two of the three years. As a senior, I was all-state. That year I was captain of the high school team and also captain of the all-state team. Football has been a major aspect of my life.

"I got the award as the most promising freshman (at Michigan). I was selected by teammates. Then after my senior year I played in the East-West Shrine football game. I played 58 minutes because the other center got hurt. When I got through the Michigan season and played in the two all-star games, I was written to by two (NFL coaches). They offered $200 a game, which was the going rate in those days, more or less guaranteed for 14 games. But I had an offer to go to Yale as an assistant. I could go to law school at the same time. That was something I wanted to do. I don't have any regrets."

Golden State Warriors forward Antawn Jamison

"It's a dream come true. Since I was a little kid I always dreamed about the opportunity of playing on this level, because this is the highest level you can play at. You are playing the best. With me, you are playing against your childhood dreams with Scottie Pippen and Charles Barkley and David Robinson. Those guys I used to watch when I was younger. ... To see them on TV when I was young, and now getting the opportunity to go up against them and try to beat them and things like that. That's just like a dream coming true.

"Everyday when I drive home to my house, there is a basketball court there, and sometimes I'll just pull over and see how the kids are playing the game. It brings back memories of me out there. Having a dream of one day I'll be able to play in the NBA and going up against the world champions or something like that. For me to pull up and see those kids still having that dream and still doing the things that I did when I was young ... that brings back the memories of my childhood.

"I see a couple jerseys (with my name and number). That's the ultimate prize, I can recall growing up in the Michael Jordan jersey. To see little kids wearing my jersey."

"I don't let them see me, I creep up and just look at their reactions. Kids really care about the game. You can tell; they are out there yelling, 'This is Michael Jordan doing this and doing that.' I can recall I used to do that also. In the backyard I was Scottie Pippen 24/7. I was doing it all. Just to creep up and not be noticed and the see the kids and the love and passion they have for the game of basketball, it reminds me of who I am right now. I'm 24, but in the heart I'm still a kid and still love the game. I still love going up against guys like Tim Duncan and Kevin Garnett, who I admire.

Colorado Avalanche goalie Patrick Roy

"My brothers and I wanted to play hockey when we were growing up in Montreal, but my mom thought the sport was too rough. She made us take swimming lessons, day after day. We had to pass the rink on the way to the pool and one day we decided to skip swimming and play hockey. That happened several days in the row before my mom found out. Boy, was she mad. At first we couldn't reason with her. Finally, she saw she couldn't keep us away from hockey, so she made a deal with us that we could play hockey as long as we continued the swimming lessons. I never became a lifeguard, but skipping those lessons did help me make a pretty nice career out of hockey."

Texas forward Chris Owens

"It was kind of strange, but in high school I started realizing just how much I love playing the game. I just felt like I wanted to win more than the others around me. ... I remember playing pick-up ball at a local park back home. It's called Crawford Park. When games are going on, there's always a lot of guys sitting around on the hoods of cars and talking a lot of noise. The first time I went there I was like 10 and I went with a bunch of my friends. I was really nervous to go out there, I had more butterflies than I get now playing in front of a big crowd. I mean, it was pretty physical and there used to be fights, a lot of tension. Let's just say there weren't many guys out there who were planning on going to college, if you know what I mean. The games were 4-on-4 and we'd play to 12, winners stay on the court. Guys would argue for 10 minutes over a call because they didn't want to lose and have to leave the court. The first night I ever went there, I got there around 7 and stayed till 10 and I only got to play once. But I kept going back.

"One of my biggest highlights in basketball came the first time I dunked on someone at Crawford Park. There was this guy who was talking trash the whole night and he was making me really mad, but I didn't say anything. I was under the rim and there was a missed shot and the ball bounced off the rim and I went up and dunked over that guy. That's when I started to feel like I belonged and could play.

"I still play there some when I go back home. They know me now, so they don't try and take my head off anymore."

New Jersey Devils defenseman Scott Stevens

"You know where I got that mean streak I have? From my brothers, Mike and Geoff. They used to try to play tricks on me and then lock me in our bedroom. I kept knocking the doors in and my parents would keep buying stronger and stronger doors to keep me from breaking them down. It never worked and finally mom and dad had to take the door down completely. Maybe I would have had a better chance at being a cop and barging through doors to catch criminals like they do on TV, but in a way my brothers helped me become a hockey player who would never let a door or obstacle get in my way.

"When I was young, my dad told me there is no such thing as a half-of-a-hit, that if you don't completely rub him out, he has a chance to get back into the play. That's why I try to make the opponent feel the hit. I feel sort of like a bolt of lightning and want to make the hit feel electric up and down his body."

New York Jets free safety Damien Robinson

"(I first realized I loved the game) when I was 5, playing Pop Warner football. But the love comes from watching the Tony Dorsetts, the Drew Pearsons, the guys in superstar roles. ... One year, we were undefeated and we playing the national pee-wee championship in Orlando. That was real big. I played tailback, receiver."

New Mexico basketball coach Fran Fraschilla

"This is the only thing I've ever wanted to do. I knew at 13 I wanted to be a college basketball coach. I got all my Christmas bonus money from being a paper boy and I went to Madison Square Garden by myself, took the train into the city, and I went to a consolation doubleheader for the Holiday Festival. I had great seats, because it was the consolation and there were 500 people in the arena. I went up and introduced myself to Al Attles, who'd just been named coach of the Golden State Warriors. We started talking and became friends. That got me hooked a little bit. It just has been in my blood.

"I gravitated toward coaching because I loved sports so much and wasn't the kind of athlete who was going to go very far. I coached high school JV basketball my freshman year in college, and by my senior year in college, I was an assistant coach in Division II.

"I've always loved football coaches. I'm a little like Tom Izzo in that respect. I grew up in the neighborhood, the section of Brooklyn that produced Joe Paterno, Vince Lombardi and Sam Rutigliano. I idolized the football coach at my high school. I used to fantasize about running out onto the field with my heavy overcoat before a big game.

Phoenix Coyotes right wing Claude Lemieux

"Competition and passion usually begin at home when you're growing up. For me, that competition was usually with my brother, Jocelyn (who also played in the NHL). My mom and dad were like the referees and linesmen, but this passion to compete didn't take place on the ice. It was at the dinner table, where Jocelyn and

I could never get enough of my mom's cooking. We'd actually start fighting and checking one another into the walls over a piece of toast. We made the battle personal at home and just took it to the rink as well."

New York Islanders goalie Rick DiPietro

"Growing up we always played baseball, football and basketball. One day, the guys said we should try hockey. Wow! What a blast! You had the hand-to-eye coordination of baseball, the hitting of football and the stops-and-starts stamina of basketball. I thought to myself, 'Why should I fool around with the other sports when hockey gives me all of the best of the other sports?' And now that I've changed from forward to goaltending, I can still use my aggressiveness by beating forwards into the corner and handling the puck better than any other goaltender."

Arizona Diamondbacks pitcher Curt Schilling

"One of the big stories that circulated in my family is that when my mom brought me home from the hospital my dad had a ball and glove in my crib.

"I can remember the day Roberto Clemente died (Schilling was 6) was about the only time I ever saw my father cry. ... I can remember Omar Moreno catching the last out of the 1979 World Series (when the Pirates beat the Orioles), and sticking my hand in the ceiling fan when I was jumping up and down.

"A lot of things in the way I approach the game were things that my dad taught me when I was very young. I was 11 years old watching the Cubs on WGN and my dad was talking about leadoff walks and first-pitch strikes, which was fun. When you're 14 years old, usually the last thing you want to do is talk about infield defenses and guys being pitched a certain way. We talked about that stuff."

Former baseball player Cookie Rojas

"I've played since I was 4, 5 years old, and I enjoyed the game so much I just wanted to keep on playing. I don't think there is any better game than this. It's a great thing, playing all the time, going out just hitting the ball, catching the ball, running the bases. In the islands, where we come from—Cuba, Puerto Rico, the Dominican Republic—the biggest sport there all year round is baseball, because of the weather. The kids are not as big or as strong as the

American kids, to play basketball or football, so our game was baseball. I always loved the game. I couldn't even think about another sport. In Canada, hockey is the biggest game because the weather is just perfect for that. In our country, it was baseball, so I grew up with it, enjoyed it, and wanted to play professionally."

Anaheim Angels shortstop David Eckstein

"Ever since I was young, I was watching baseball all the time. When I was 4 years old I was a batboy for my brother's team. ... (My friends and I) played every day after school, and when I talk to them now, they're always giving me challenges. Like if a left-hander gets me out, I'll always get a call from one friend because he was a lefthanded pitcher."

Philadelphia Phillies outfielder Doug Glanville

"One thing I really enjoy about the game is all kinds of different people from different walks of life. They're all trying to play togeth-er with that one common goal. That's why baseball's always a step ahead in our own country in how people relate to each other—and I think that's an admirable quality. Not that it was perfect, but when

I was growing up (in Teaneck, N.J.), we had a lot of diversity, and people at least seemed to talk. That's the way it is in baseball. People are from all walks of life, and I enjoy that part, I really do.

"It was early that I realized I love playing baseball. My older brother (Kenny) played, and I always liked to do what he did. I played Strat-o-Matic, I played baseball on the computer, and I played in the summers. I had the old Apple, 'Star League' baseball. It was a great game. I always enjoyed it."

New York Yankees first baseman Jason Giambi

"I don't even know how old I was, because I was so young when I began to love baseball. I always had a bat in my hand, even when I was in a crib. My dad passed it on, and I ran with it. That's all I did—T-ball, Whiffleball, whatever, anything, I just loved to be out there. I never even thought about doing anything else. When all the other kids said they wanted to be firemen or police-men, I always said baseball player. That's it. I don't even know what else I would do; I'm not qualified for anything else.

"Baseball was the only thing I was interested in. ... I liked football, but I hated practicing all the time just to play one game a week. I loved basketball, but I never saw me guarding Allen Iverson. There was not even a doubt in my mind—all I ever wanted to be was this. I don't think there are many 11-year-olds taking batting practice for fun, but that's what I did all the time. And I never went on summer vacation, I was always playing on a team, but I never felt like I was missing out. That was exactly what I wanted to do."

Boston Red Sox outfielder Johnny Damon

"When I was little, I remember realizing that every time I took the field, I did something good. When you hit .750 in Little League, you tend to be better than everyone else. That's what kept me going—I always wanted to hit .750. ... It's a child's game, and everyone loves baseball. It doesn't matter your race or size or age, anyone can play it—that's why the game has survived so much turmoil."

NASCAR driver Kevin Harvick

"It's what I've wanted to do ever since I was a kid. When I was offered a ride at 17, I scrapped the idea of becoming an architect and left college to pursue my dream. My dad got me into rac-

ing, he worked on cars all his life."

Boston Red Sox pitcher Pedro Martinez

"When I was around 14, me and my brother Nelson were play-

ing so often and practicing so often and we were so hooked into it,

whenever I had extra hour from high school, I would skip it and just

go to the field. Sometimes I'd go in uniform—we'd have to wear blue

jeans and blue shirt, the high school colors—and I would go in uni-

form and get it dirty that day, and then wear it the next day, because

wouldn't have time to go home and pick up my clothes. ... Baseball

was like everything. Every little time I had was for baseball. I don't

think I was dreaming about it, but I was so into baseball, there was

nothing else for me. Baseball and school, baseball and school."

Former Colorado State defensive back Justin Gallimore

"At 9 is when I first realized I loved the game. After your first

touchdown, your first tackle, that's when you truly love it. Hearing

the parents cheer and knowing you actually beat someone else for

that play."

New York Mets pitcher Al Leiter

"What got me into baseball was growing up with five older brothers, me being the baby. Every single one of us from the oldest down played baseball. Loved it. Ate, slept and drank baseball. ... I do remember getting together all the time with siblings and friends and neighbors. That's something that I think is lost a little bit today, unfortunately. Kids have other interests. Perhaps the game has suffered or may suffer for it."

Former baseball player Bobby Bonilla

"I went to a lot of the Mets and Yankees games. I was kind of a New York fan, more toward the Mets' side. You kind of root for the underdog at the time. But I enjoyed going to Yankees games and Mets games. One of the things I used to love doing was buying a scorecard and keeping score. I absolutely had a passion for it. I actually just did it the other day. I still had a lot of fun. I remembered everything. I did everything. It was a good time. It actually keeps you in the game. It keeps you from drifting. It's just fun to keep score at a baseball game. It's something I can't wait to do with my son. You know, teach him how to do it and explain to him about it. It's just a lot of fun."

Seattle Seahawks defensive lineman John Randle

"As a kid growing up, I didn't really have a lot of friends. I never really fit in with a lot of people. So I started playing football. It was like the guys I was around didn't fit the norm, either. They had big feet and this and that. I stuck with it, and I got better at it. It's just that I love it. It's been good. I'm still good at it right now and I know that. I love playing the game, just having fun out there.

"There are not too many other jobs in this world where they get to scream and holler, chase guys around, tackle guys and you and 50 or 60 other guys are playing together and competing. It's fun.

"It happened real early. I was very active as a kid. I used to sweat a lot. There weren't too many things that were it for me. I tried basketball, and that wasn't it. It was football. I guess it was at age 5 or 6, playing in the backyard. I knew that was it then. But I didn't start playing organized football until I got to ninth grade. But by that time, I knew that's what I wanted to do."

Pittsburgh Steelers strong safety Lee Flowers

"I think I realized that I loved it and was pretty good at it in eighth grade when I scored my first touchdown, just the thrill and the rush that I got and just the love that the fans gave me, I was like, 'This is something I wouldn't mind for a long time.'"

Philadelphia Flyers right winger Rick Tocchet

"Hockey is in your blood as a young kid in Canada. A lot of kids do it and you kind of become a product of the environment and then after a while it just becomes a part of your blood. Hockey Night In Canada, the cold weather outside, and road hockey ... There's just a passion for it as a kid you want to be an NHL player.

"When I was 5, I was dreaming that one day I'd like to be playing on Saturday nights in front of millions of people. It was great thinking about it as a kid."

Detroit Lions CEO and president and former NFL player and broadcaster Matt Millen

"I can remember I started playing when I was 8 years old. But I can remember when I was 10, trying to draw up—I can still remember the plays: 22 Smash, 34 Counter. I can remember those plays. I was 10 years old and I would draw them up on a piece of paper and my brother had this game with little football players on a field, and

I would set them all up, and then I would move the players accordingly. I loved that part of it. I loved seeing if everybody was blocked, where or who could be the guy that got me, because I was a running back when I was little. It just made sense to me in my mind. So I guess at an early age I knew that I really loved it."

Former NFL player Andy Russell

"I can remember growing up as a youngster. Like every kid, I would get involved in pickup football games in a field or a backyard. And I loved making people miss me. I was a running back in college, and I always loved the thrill or playing the game. I'm probably much like anybody, but I don't remember one specific incident where I said (I love this). When I played high school football, I didn't really think about college. I just thought about doing the best I could in high school. When I got to college, I didn't think about pro. I never considered playing pro. I just kept going to those different levels, and I loved it."

CBS broadcaster and former NFL player Craig James

"(I remember) when I was a little boy, 5, 6, 7 and 8 years old, playing pickup football in the neighborhood with boys who were the same age and some who were older. Taking my shoes off, playing tackle football and couldn't wait until the next game. Getting holes in my socks, knees worn out on my pants, grass stains and getting in trouble when I got home and I couldn't wait to play the next time. And, nobody could bring me down, and I said, 'OK, I like this sport.' Even the bigger guys ... they had a hard time wrestling me to the ground. I took a strong desire to the game when I was young, man. When pee-wee football started, I was all over it.

"In terms of the passion for the game, I was very fortunate in that the best team I ever played on was my high-school team my senior year. We went 15-0, won the state championship in Texas. It was awesome, the chemistry, the love for each other and the passion to play on Friday night. If I could go back and play one year, that would be it, relive it one more time. And I played on two Cotton Bowl SWC championship teams, I played in a Super Bowl, and those were fun, but nothing like the thrill of being with the guys I'd grown up with as 16-, 17- and 18-year-olds in the huddle. That was the ultimate."

CHAPTER 2

Introductions

Introductions

There was a day and age when game-day introductions consisted of a few courtesy claps and a tip of the cap. Today they're no small event.

But for athletes then and now, the crowd reaction is only part of the story. Introductions are psych-up sessions, time for the players to put their games into motion.

It's game on.

Introductions

New York Jets running back Curtis Martin

"When you're in the locker room before the game starts, and you're sitting there and there's still silence, almost like a silence sweeping over the locker room. You don't know what it is. You can look in the eyes of your teammates. Sometimes you get to see the other team. A lot of times I look in their eyes. You can see fear. You can see excitement. You can see nervousness. It's that before-the-game moment. In my mind, it's like everything is silent. It's like another realm, another world. It's like, 'This is it, it's all on the line.' For me, every game, it's all on the line. Just that little moment, knowing it's all on the line, right now, there's no second chance on this game, there's no getting a play over, that's something that excites me. I love to see other players, especially defenders, if they're nervous. Yeah, that gets me excited."

Former Colorado State defensive back Jason Gallimore

"Thursday night games are amazing because it's national TV. The police escorts on the buses are something that stick with me. You start to think: 'Wow, this really means something.' Walking through the middle of the stadium before a game, looking at the empty stands and how big it is. That's when I'm caught up in the moment. Looking at the vastness of it all."

Former Northwestern running back Damien Anderson

"Being in the huddle, right before we go out for a series is a great feeling. I know we've prepared and that we're ready. The thing that sticks out the most for me, I don't know how many times, is the first series of the game. That's when I get the biggest rush. It's time again. It calms you and puts things in perspective. You are well-prepared and it's time to show every-one."

NFL defensive back Blaine Bishop

"I would say the rush of just running out. The nervous feeling that you feel running out at the beginning of the game and getting that first hit out of the way. And, then you're relaxed and ready to play football. That's like a little thing you just can't wait every game for that to happen. I try to get it out of way real quick. Sometimes it takes longer than others, but I try to get it out of the way real quick."

Stanford guard/forward Casey Jacobsen

"I love the huddle before the game. If you really think about it, the huddle is one of the most remarkable examples of together-ness you can find anywhere. There are men from all different backgrounds, races, experiences and beliefs that are all trying to work together toward one common goal. The huddle is where I realize that I belong to something really special. That something is bigger than any one individual and its bigger than any win or loss."

New York Jets free safety Damien Robinson

"It's the feeling you get on game day, driving through the tailgaters in the parking lot—the whole pre-game atmosphere. You can see it, hear it and smell it. I always notice that. As a player, it lets you know that people really appreciate the game. People getting there early, seeing you walk through the tunnel and asking for your autograph. Just being out there that early in the morning, tailgating, you know they have to love the game like we do."

Colorado quarterback Craig Ochs

"A special time for me is running behind Ralphie into Folsom. There's about a five-minute lull when I throw in warmups before the game starts. During that time, the fans are loud. The stadium is full. The other team is out. It's sort of the calm before the storm. That's the time when you get to take it all in. During a game, I'm too focused to notice. But I do notice it then, and that's what college football is all about."

Mississippi quarterback Eli Manning

"I'm passionate about the preparation. Each week, it's starting over with a new opponent. Getting in there on a Sunday and watching film. The whole process of getting to know each team, who their best players are and what they do well. It's always a different challenge. ... I also love the feeling of running through that tunnel before games. You're nervous, you're excited."

Tennessee Titans offensive lineman Brad Hopkins

"For me, it's the introductions. The introductions to an NFL football game are probably something that very few people will experience in this world. To actually be part of an NFL team and being introduced as a starter, and just seeing all the people there on the edge of their seats ready for an exciting, riveting game, and just cheering you on when you run through that row of players out to your team, and the roar of the crowd and just the whole energy that's created within the stadium that really makes it come to life what it is you're doing. Having the success that we've had going to the Super Bowl and winning championships as far as the AFC. Being in big games like that and having those type of crowds and that type of energy—it just transforms through your whole body when you're going out there for the game."

Former LSU linebacker Trev Faulk

"We walk down the hill to our stadium. That's a great moment and one reason why I love this game. Seeing all of our fans out there hours before the game to support us is a great feeling. You see your family, your friends, your fellow classmates. On our bus ride over, you see lots of mobile homes and people tailgating. Then, when you walk through the goal posts, it's an unbelievable experience. It gives you goose bumps."

Wisconsin quarterback Brooks Bollinger

"It's special every time you run out in Camp Randall with everyone going crazy. That feeling when you're about to start the game, and you know all the work you've put in, and the team on the other side has done the exact same thing. That point is pretty intense. That's a special time."

Arizona Cardinals quarterback Jake Plummer

"I'd say definitely standing in the tunnel ready to be introduced. That kind of quiet before the storm. I don't get all hyped, smash helmets and punch this guy and that. I just kind of stand there and soak in all the energy coming from these guys.

"When it hit me the most is when I was injured and missed a couple of games and then got introduced again. You almost tear up. The emotions are running high. That's one of the sights and sounds I love, at the beginning. You get to look at each player in the eye and you know right away by looking at them who's ready to go to war that day."

Indianapolis Colts quarterback Peyton Manning

"As a quarterback playing in the National Football League, when you're playing at home or go out on the road, and you run out for warm-ups and hear them call your name 'Peyton Manning, University of Tennessee,' that's a great feeling and something that I never take for granted and always look forward to. When you go on the road and they introduce you and the crowd boos you, even that is kind of a unique feeling. You truly know that you're not just playing against the Jets' defense, but every fan in that stadium as well. It makes you even more challenged. I'm certainly very aware of the crowd, you can hear them in warm-ups and during the game on third down when they're getting louder and louder, you are certainly very aware of them and it makes you focus a little more."

St. Louis Rams wide receiver Torry Holt

"I like the feeling on Sundays when you wake up in the morning and you put on that nice suit or those nice slacks or whatever is comfortable for you going to the game. Having that good breakfast and your car is clean and you've got your nice music, whether it's gospel or rap, to prepare you for that competition. I just love that feeling, it's like building up for the Fourth of July as a little kid when you want to see those fireworks every year, going back to that particular amusement park, you know you're going to get the same fireworks that will just light you soul up. I look forward to it, that's how I look forward to sundays, that adrenaline rush is just unbelievably out of control. It brings tears to my eyes."

Pro Football Hall of Famer Steve Largent

"Sitting on the training table and getting your ankles taped up is special. ... The very intense and almost somber sort of atmosphere that exists just prior to the game, when you want nothing more than just to go out there and hit somebody or get hit for the first time to kind of relieve the pressure or stress that you feel before the game starts."

Kentucky point guard J.P. Blevins

"To me, college basketball is about the adrenaline that you feel. Before a ballgame, whether it's on the road or at home, you're kind of walking on a cloud; you're in a different zone. There's all the pressure, plus you're doing what you love to do and dreamed of doing your whole life. All your friends are watching, the crowd is roaring, and there's an electricity about the place—and about you—that really is the most exciting thing to me."

St. Joseph's point guard Jameer Nelson

"Being around my teammates in the locker room before the

game. I see everybody preparing for the game ... most of them are listening to music, and you've got others that want to joke around. I do a little of both. It depends on what type of mood I'm in. I don't really have a routine. You just know that the game is about to come. That's what you practice for, that's what you work for, and you're ready for the challenge."

Georgia offensive tackle Jon Stinchcomb

"Look around and see all those fans who are there for you, to watch your team perform. It's really something special. This past year's Tennessee game, with everyone storming the field. The electricity that ran through the stadium the entire game is a memory that will stay with me my whole life."

Orlando Magic point guard Darrell Armstrong

"The day I came from overseas for my first NBA game, I had played in Madrid the night before. I flew in from Madrid to New York. ... I was in shorts because I left from Madrid, but it was cold in Philly and I was freezing my tail off. The first two players I meet when I go to the locker room are Shaquille O'Neal and Horace

Grant, and they were the two biggest guys I ever met. To walk out and go shoot around with those guys for the first time was amazing. I can remember thinking how funny it was I wore the same shoes I wore the night before in Spain, and then here I am warming up at The Spectrum the next night. It was amazing to see that gym and see that arena when I walked in. It was an unbelievable feeling. I just couldn't believe it. Right then and there, that let me know I had made it."

Former Minnesota Twins coach and baseball player Paul Molitor

"You'd go into the ballparks, whether it was the old ones like Yankee Stadium and Fenway, or the new ones like Camden and Jacobs and you'd come off the field from batting practice and you'd have five or 10 minutes before you took the infield, and you'd just kind of sit on the top step and look around at the people and the atmosphere and you watch the ball being fired around the field, and the anticipation you'd feel every night waiting for that first pitch ... those are things as a player that reminded me how great it was to be able to put that uniform on every day."

Anaheim Angels outfielder Darin Erstad

"There's something about taping up, about tying your shoes ... when I tie my shoes before a game, it's like a light turns on for me. I haven't tried to figure it out. I just know it's there."

CHAPTER 3

Senses

Senses

You know it's love because everything is magnified and intensified. The nerve sensors are on operating on a hair-trigger and your love activates them in every way.

You look for things in your love that others can't see. You listen for what others never hear. Your love has a smell that is instantly recognized and identified by your brain. You associate certain tastes with your love. You feel things for your love that others can't feel.

Sports are an emotional and passionate experience that activate the all the senses of those who not only live it, but love it.

Senses

Baseball Hall of Famer and Kansas City Royals vice president of baseball operations George Brett

"When you go into Dodger Stadium and you can smell those Dodger Dogs from about a half a mile out. ... 99 percent of the times when I go to a game I've got to get a hot dog, it's just something about going to a sporting event, you need a hot dog and a beer. Unfortunately, when I go to a game now I'm working, so there's no beer. But, if I go to a Chiefs game, yeah, I'll have a beer. ... It's just the beauty of it. God, we just put down a new infield, new sod in the infield and it looks like a pool table. it's beautiful. It's a beautiful sunny afternoon, it's probably 80 degrees out and the wind blowing slightly out to left. And some big thunderheads or cumulus stratus clouds in the sky. And it's just a perfect day for baseball."

Former Tennessee defensive end Will Overstreet

"I love the game because it's the only one where you can run through somebody. You can get out frustration and all the bad things in the back of your head. It's like therapy. You always want to be the guy who takes over a game. Knowing you're the best is something everyone thrives for. ... When you make a great play, everything slows down. You can see it all happen, everything is happening in slow motion. And then once the play is over, everything speeds up and is back to normal. It's hard to describe. It's the best feeling in the world. You know it's about to happen, and it happens."

Former LSU linebacker Trev Faulk

"I love the contact of the game. Even if I get hit hard, I pat the guy on the back and tell him 'good job.' I also like to blow a guy up. When one of my teammates makes a big hit, I'm the first one there, jumping around and yelling about it."

NASCAR driver Mark Martin

"Anyone who has there favorite spot on the couch or knows what it feels like to sit in their favorite easy chair at home or wherever it is, they know what I'm talking about. When I slip into my car, it always feels like I'm sitting in my favorite chair. It's just that comfortable."

Wisconsin quarterback Brooks Bollinger

"I love this game when it is close, and both teams have been going back and forth, and you get down late in the contest. It's the time when the game will be decided. That's when you don't have time to think about it. You don't get that feeling very often. I don't think I can describe it. It's not one of butterflies because you are so involved in the game. At the moment, you don't have time to feel it. Afterward, you say, 'Geez, that was a great moment.' It's like when you're in the zone. Everything is kind of blocked out and if things are going right, everything else is in slow motion and you are a step ahead."

Kentucky point guard J.P. Blevins

"When you get cold chills before a ballgame, you know you're doing something special. College basketball is so special because it can provide that. I don't know if NBA guys are getting cold chills before they play.

"A basketball is a basketball. When you're playing in front of 24,000 people, and you're nervous and your blood is pumping, and there are all these things going on around you, like maybe an SEC division title game—when you get hold of that basketball, it's the same as when you were in the backyard at six or seven. The ball brings you back to what you're doing; you kind of forget about everything else. It's just a basketball, a simple round ball, and yet so many people get so much out of college basketball. And yet it all comes down to this little round ball, which is just like any other ball you'd ever grab. It makes you feel a lot more comfortable. Before the game you start patting it around, shooting it; it gets you in a more relaxed state. 'OK, I've felt this ball 10 million times.'"

Former Pittsburgh defensive end Bryan Knight

"There is nothing better than making a big tackle behind the line of scrimmage. Not a shoestring tackle. I'm talking pads on pads. Just having that player wrapped up and feeling yourself taking him down to the ground. All year, you work out and study. And in just one play, everything pays off. When you make that sack, there is no better feeling in the world."

Dallas Cowboys fullback Robert Thomas

"I like the pain that comes with the pain. I like the fatigue. And the bruises. And the soreness because it forces you to fight yourself and the pain and play ball. It brings you closer to your teammates, when everybody is fighting through the pain of the game to win.

"I love to feel a linebacker cringe, when I run into him and hear him make a funny noise. I love to see the fear in another man's eyes. ... I love to make another man quit. If you can play with pain and through pain, then you become a champion.

"The game has its own unique smell. It's not sweat or the funk from the equipment, it's a strange smell that's hard to describe.

Maybe it's the smell of fear because football is a barbaric sport, where 22 men come together to chase a pigskin."

Philadelphia Phillies outfielder Doug Glanville

"There are a lot of things to love, the smells and sounds of the game. ... Hitting a home run is a great part of the game. They don't happen too often, so you have to enjoy them. It's a chance to get that crispy sound. Sometimes you foul a ball back, and you get that wood-burning sensation. When you hit it right, it's something else, it really is."

Oakland Raiders fullback Jon Ritchie

"For anyone who is a medium guy like myself, there are the big guys like the offensive lineman and the defensive lineman, and there's like the little guys like defensive backs and wide receivers and sometimes quarterbacks are thrown in there, but medium guys like linebackers and running backs usually have the glorious task of head-to-head collisions, in my opinion, but maybe I have a biased viewpoint. I think at an early age, if you discover that you have medium-guy build you learn to appreciate the merits of collisions. It's different, every collision is like a story with a different ending. Every block, if you're a fullback, has limitless possibilities. If you're a linebacker on defense, every block that you shed and tackle is like a story in itself. Because there are two people involved, both have a separate agenda and both are doing their best to get the best of their one-on-one opponent. So it's kind of like a choreography of aggression, which ends with one person beating another. The beauty of that is there are all kinds of side effects involved, like the loss of vision from a head-to-head collision. You can either have the loss of vision or super-intense vision where everything gets really, really bright for a couple seconds or you can have the little floater vision where there are little stars, like translucent orbs circling in front of your eyes.

"As far as smell goes with a collision, if you get hit hard enough it's like you can smell the pain. I got so jacked by Junior Seau on a little checkdown over the middle where he just kind of caught me at a great angle when my head was turned. I could smell this acrid, putrid, I didn't even know what it was or where that scent came from, but it was like the smell of ... shock.

"Junior made me smell pain on that play, but there's always the rest of the game to try to balance the scales. Regardless, Junior Seau is a guy who will be immortalized as one of the greatest linebackers ever to play the game. Going into a game against him is a real, real challenge to get the better of those collisions. That's the beauty of this sport: week to week and even day to day in practice you never know what to expect from your combatant, the guy that you're going up against one on one. He has an array of techniques and moves and abilities that are different from the next guy. No matter how well you might have done on one play, you're always set up for disappointment on the next play."

NASCAR driver Kyle Petty

"There's just something about everything at the racetrack. It doesn't make any difference. The smell of the track is sometimes like a state fair more so than a racetrack. It's more like a carnival, like a roadshow. And it's the people. It's like walking down through the garage area at Charlotte Motor Speedway and seeing the same people you see at Daytona and at California. And it's almost like you feel like you've come back home. You are just comfortable in that environment."

Marshall basketball coach Greg White

"It's the locker room, the smell, the different looks in different arenas. It's the butterflies that go with putting on a uniform and the locker room preparations as a coach."

Pittsburgh Steelers strong safety Lee Flowers

"Freshly cut grass to me, reminds me of training camp. It reminds me when the grounds crew is keeping the grounds fresh for you because you are going through two-a-days and they got to keep cutting the grass four or five times week. Just the smell of freshly cut grass to me sends a chill through my body because I know it's always time to go back to work. It's summer time and training camp is coming up and it's time to start going back to work, and that's when I really start getting pumped up."

Minnesota Twins infielder Denny Hocking

"The smell of fresh cut grass always sticks out. Playing at

home here on turf, you don't get to smell that. I love that part about being on the road. … The sight of sitting in Yankee Stadium watching an old-timers' game, with a Ralph Houk or Clete Boyer in your dugout, being able to say 'Hi,' to those guys, that's a tremendous feeling. Just getting a chance to learn more about the people who paved the way to where I am today is exciting. … As far as hearing, I love it when Kirby (Puckett) comes into our clubhouse and stirs it up. He still does that a lot. It's nice, because he's still a very integral part of our organization. He has a tremendous effect on a lot of the guys in this clubhouse. You can be in a slump and he'll come in and say, 'What are you doing? Why don't you get up there and swing the bat?' And you're like, 'Gosh, he's watching. Maybe I'll take his advice.'"

Anaheim Angels outfielder Darin Erstad

"For me it's the competition, the camaraderie with my teammates, the smell of pine tar … Pine tar is on your bats, your glove. I just associate the smell of it with baseball. It's part of the build up to the game. You have to have the right amount on your bat, mixed with the right amount of resin.

"Back home in North Dakota, we had four months a year where the weather was good enough to play. Our season was 2½ months long. We were out from sun up to sun down playing baseball every day. It was such a precious time, from the time I was seven years old.

"It's the process. You're working on your glove, fixing your bat up so you're ready to go. The game itself is the fun part, when you can lose yourself for three hours, the feeling you have when you're completely into something. It's something I'm not going to have 15-20 years from now.

"After a win and your uniform is all dirty and you feel like you've helped the team ... that's a great feeling. To get to do something you've wanted to do since you were a little kid ... nothing else can beat that.

"Hockey is the same type of thing, the competition, lacing up your skates and taping your stick, putting on your smelly old equipment. There are certain smells; every rink has its own odor. It's like that in baseball, too. I grew up with the smell of the Metrodome, the smell of hot dogs is what I remember."

Oakland Raiders team executive and Pro Football Hall of Famer Jim Otto

"The smell of the grass. The cool autumn air. It's something I've smelled since I was a little boy and it all relates to football. You know, you smell the grass, fresh cut grass on the field. I can remember the stickum that the players would wear, I never wore it, but you could smell that it was like a pine tar smell along with the grass and the autumn air."

NFL defensive end Michael McCrary

"I play this game each week because it's worth going out on the field and seeing the uncertainty in a grown man's eyes. That's the only reason I play. ... I love hitting a quarterback and hearing the air escape from his lungs, and it's only the second play of the game and he knows it."

Kansas point guard Kirk Hinrich

"I love warming up and listening to the band. One team on this end, one team on the other. You're just really excited. Then you're back in the locker room and Coach (Roy Williams) is giving his little motivational talk, and you're getting ready to run out in front of thousands of people, you're getting a little nerv-

ous. It's just a great feeling. There's nothing like the college

atmosphere."

Virginia Tech cornerback Ronyell Whitaker

"Making a big play, like an interception, is special to me. To

hear the crowd roar. While the play is going on, everyone is quiet.

But once you get the interception, especially when you take it to

the house, just to hear the roar of the crowd get louder and loud-

er the closer you get to the end zone. And then coming over to

the sideline to celebrate with your teammates and coaches. It's the

best thing for me."

St. Louis Rams wide receiver Torry Holt

"When I catch a nice pass on third-and-10 and we convert for

the first down, and you hear that crowd cheering and screaming.

You might hear somebody say, (his voice goes up) 'Great job,

Torry, great catch!' You kind of get that feeling like, 'Wow, they

really appreciate what I did right there.' I like the feeling of that.

I like to hear the fans and that I'm giving them exactly what it is they came to see."

Detroit Lions CEO and president and former NFL player and broadcaster Matt Millen

"Most of what we talk about is sight, but a player who is in tune, will have a good sense of sound, of hearing. You can hear the difference on a lot of plays.

"There are smells, that I'll go by or pass, and there's a smell of a locker room, there's the smell of the fresh-cut grass, the smell of the morning practice, there's the smell of all those things.

"But probably sight and sound are the most on-the-field, because you can really hear. You can hear an offense not breathing before a quick-count. You can hear the offense, and the difference on a play-action pass and a run. You can hear the difference if you're listening for it. You can hear the difference when you're working with a guy one-on-one and he's running an individual route, anticipate when he's going to make a break based on how he breathes. You can hear it. And, if you are aware of it, you can use it as a help.

"So, there are a lot of things, that if I said this to the normal person, they'd think, 'You're goofy.' But to those of us who have played at that level, when you stop and think about it, 'You know what,' you go, 'Hey, he's right.'

"I would teach young players you can hear the difference in a play, between play-action and a run play. You can hear it. You can hear the snap count, linemen come up and all of sudden when it's a quick count, right before the quarterback comes up there's a pause and they hold their breath. Just like a dog. If you have a dog, and he hears a sounds, he'll sit up and he'll stop breathing and he'll listen. It's the same thing for linemen. It's really kind of neat."

Connecticut basketball coach Jim Calhoun

"To me, basketball is a sport where you're basically exposed to the world. I say football is a spectator sport and a field sport, basketball is a living room sport. People can see you breath. They can see the sweat. They can hear you and feel you. You don't have a face mask to protect you if you make a bad play. ... It's just a game that's in your blood, and I think that if I hear a ball bouncing, I look up."

Minnesota Twins infielder Denny Hocking

"I'll always remember seeing the Green Monster, and seeing all the dents in there and I've hit it one time in a game, so I know I've got a mark on that wall. That's history. I know it's only one, and Nomar's probably got a hundred, but it's kind of cool to me."

Former Minnesota Twins coach and baseball player Paul Molitor

"It's a little different now as a coach that I don't play anymore. ... Now as a coach, trying to pass on some of the things you've learned, and watching young players figure things out and developing, that's where I get my reward. I still have the love, because you see other young people now as you pass the torch doing the same things you did as a player."

Minnesota Twins bullpen coach Rick Stelmaszek

"I think every ballpark and every city has their own little characteristics. We go to a place like Baltimore, and they've got the new stadium, but re-done in the old way with a lot of wrought iron, green, with the smell of Boog Powell's beef and onions in right field. Going onto the field at 4:30, instead of throwing a baseball you want him to throw you one of those sandwiches he's making over there. That jumps out at you.

"Every stadium, every ball park has that little something special about it. The older ballparks have the stickiness, the stale smell of beer, the small locker rooms. Fenway Park you feel the dampness of the stands and the dugout and the cold feeling that you have, but you go on the field and the Green Monster and the greenery and the closeness of the fans grabs you. You get a little charged up when you're there, with the tradition and everything else that goes with it."

Milwaukee Bucks coach George Karl

"I think the game has a power. I think it has a spirit. That power makes things better. Friendships are stronger, teamwork is more important. There's an energy that comes with the spirit of success and winning. I've been in timeouts and huddles when those hands are together, and I'll tell you there's some electricity in that 5-7 seconds when you're talking. There's something going on there."

Pittsburgh Penguins center Mario Lemieux

"There were a lot of days that I would wake up over the past four years and wonder if maybe I retired too soon. When I stepped on the ice to do a commercial with Jaromir Jagr … on how two players can really work together, I felt the joy I enjoyed for so many years. … Having the itch to play again after being off so long is a form of passion, isn't it?"

Former NHL defenseman Ray Bourque

"Hockey is all wrapped up in the transition game. I've always relished the idea of facing the game's best players—a Wayne Gretzky or Mario Lemieux or Eric Lindros. What is an even better feeling is stopping them and sending the traffic in the other direction with a good outlet pass. There are nights when I know how a good traffic cop feels, sending the traffic in one direction and another."

Toronto Blue Jays pitcher Dan Plesac

"I think there are a lot of people who can actually say they do what they love and they love what they do. I mean, I'm probably no different than any kid who grew up wanting to be a baseball player, and every day I put a uniform on, I feel the same way I did in 1986, the first time at Yankee Stadium. That is not to say there aren't some high moments and some low moments, but I can honestly say my love and respect for the game, not only for the current players now but for the players that set the tone, who made history early in baseball.

"When you go to ballparks like Yankee Stadium, Fenway Park, Wrigley Field, it's hard not to daydream about the Billy Williams, the Ernie Banks, the Carlton Fisks, the Babe Ruths, the Don Mattinglys—the guys who made those ballparks special to what they are today.

"You come into Fenway and the first thing you think seeing the Green Monster is Carlton Fisk trying to keep that ball fair in the World Series.

"I have never allowed myself to lose sight that this is a very special thing I've been allowed to do. I never in my wildest dreams thought this would last as long as it has. I probably enjoy and appreciate playing now, more so than ever. I think when you're a young player, things important to you—contracts, arbitration, financial stability, free agency—weigh heavily on your mind. It's hard for them not to become a distraction because you see the paydays that are out there. I'm not playing now for the money. I'm playing because I love what I do, I still think I can pitch at a level I'm happy with, and I enjoy the the game for what it is.

"I was sitting in the bullpen yesterday, thinking I can remember the first game I ever pitched at Fenway like it was yesterday, and here it is 16 years later. Our society today is so into everything being new, state of the art, having bells and whistles, and I just wish guys would take more opportunity to appreciate Fenway, Wrigley, Yankee Stadium for what they are. They are special places, not only for those cities, but for baseball. There's a lot of history, and I don't think enough guys step back to appreciate what a privilege it is to play in places like this. It's not a plush clubhouse with the nice carpet, big-screen TVs and cherrywood lockers like some of the new places, but there's a lot of history, a lot of heritage, and I just wish guys would take more of that in and appreciate what it is."

Anaheim Angels shortstop David Eckstein

"I love the competition, the ability to compete against another team. I like the dirt on my uniform. I love to have a dirty uniform at the end of the day. Usually, if I have a dirty uniform things have gone well that day. Turning a double play; making solid contact, the feeling you get there is very good ... it's real free-flowing when you hit the sweet spot, like it's effortless. I love the smell of popcorn ... in some parks, especially in some minor league parks, it's stronger than others. When you smell popcorn, you know it's baseball time. I also love eating popcorn, too. It brings you back to your Little League days. I love the smell of freshly cut grass, the look of a freshly manicured field, when you go out in the first inning and see everything in place."

New York Yankees first baseman Jason Giambi

"It's that feeling of being utterly at peace with myself when I'm on a baseball field. There's nothing better on the earth. When I walk on the field, that's like peace to me. Even during my divorce, the greatest thing in the world was those three hours I'd spend on the field. Just hanging out with the guys, the competition of you vs. the pitcher, everything—that's my moment when I'm at peace. It's the greatest gift in the world."

Boston Red Sox outfielder Johnny Damon

"I love the feel of the dirt under your feet; I love digging in. I feel like I'm at home."

Pittsburgh Pirates infielder Pokey Reese

"I just enjoy making plays. I enjoy going out and getting dirty. I don't like coming in after a game clean."

Cincinnati Reds pitcher Chris Reitsma

"I like the sound a fastball makes when it pounds the mitt. That kind of gives you a feeling of empowerment. It makes you feel like your hard work has paid off."

Former baseball player Willie Horton

"Cold sweat on the back of my neck in a tough situation. I go to the ballpark now and I still miss that. There are two out and a man on second with two strikes, and you just have got to get that run home. Got to work that count. Got to do the job. I had a responsibility.

"I hit a ball in Boston once that smacked right into a pigeon that was flying overhead. WHAM! I'll never forget the thudding sound when it hit him. It kind of made a splat when it landed on home plate. I took off running.

"The grass in the outfield, especially after they've just cut it. It's where I lived; it'll always be a part of my life. That smell, like all the other sensations, knows no color. It's part of our lives as people. It's part of my life forever."

Houston Astros second baseman Craig Biggio

"Walking into this ballpark (Wrigley Field), walking out to this field. Just with the tradition, it makes you feel like this is what baseball is about. I love Chicago. You have good days and bad days in baseball, but there's something about it. The Bleacher Bums, the history, the aura that's here. You kind of realize that you're playing on a field that Babe Ruth played on. It's something that's pretty cool."

Arizona Cardinals assistant coach and Pro Football Hall of Famer Mean Joe Greene

"People who are in sports can walk out on to the field and just feel it, before anything is ever done, before any ball is ever kicked. Feel the environment."

Former Colorado State defensive back Justin Gallimore

"I like the big hit, looking down at your opponent. And the sound of the crowd after you've delivered a hit is neat. There is nothing that can replace that. You watch the TV version and turn up the sound to hear the crowd and how excited it gets after a play you make."

Former Colorado State defensive back Jason Gallimore

"During the course of a game, you can experience every emotion. You cry, bleed, sweat, you exert every type of energy. You are happy, disappointed. And just competing and giving everything you have to beat that person."

Georgia offensive tackle Jon Stinchcomb

"Some of the best advice I got was my freshman year when we were in Knoxville playing Tennessee. Coach said to be sure to take a minute during the game to look around and realize the type of environment we get to play in. It's unlike any other. I also apply that advice for every home game at Sanford Stadium.

"I don't think there's a better feeling in the world than making a good block, whether it's pancaking a defensive lineman or running off a linebacker and driving him for 10, 15 yards and that block leading to hole where the running back breaks it and scores a touchdown. Just playing a key role on a play that helps your team out on a large scale. It's moments like that that make all of the blood, sweat and tears worth it."

Cincinnati Bengals linebacker Takeo Spikes

"Hitting gives me that extra oomph. I dream of that clean shot, coming from the blind side and just killing somebody or going through somebody just to get to the ball carrier. I won't be denied. That's how I think. I do whatever it takes to get to the ball. I dream of hitting a running back so hard that his helmet comes off.

Then I pick up the helmet and throw it to the head coach. I think about that. I really do. That drives me. ... It's all in the eyes. I not only want him to see pain, I want him to feel it. That's worth 15 yards.

"I try to get down and get a good feel for what's going on. I look at the formation. I look into the running back's eyes and I look into the quarterback's eyes. I even go as far as looking into the guard's eyes, just to see where he's going. A lot of times, they'll tilt and let you know which way they're going. I can tell when the quarterback keeps looking and flinching at you, or the fullback keeps looking at you ... I just know it's time to load up.

"I want them to think, 'Oh, (crap), he's for real.' Speak without even speaking, where they can look at each other and say, 'He's for real, so you better bring it.' I want them to say, 'Coach, don't call that play on that side. Just call it on the other side.'

"(The) ability to go out and take anger out on somebody without getting in trouble for it. I want to hit him so that, when he gets up, he may talk noise because it's a man thing to do, but deep in his eyes, you see fear. He'll give you that look like, 'He's for real. He's packing it.' He'll get on his fullback and say, 'Don't let that guy come in here clean.' That's what I like. That's gas in the tank."

Pro Football Hall of Famer Steve Largent

"When I think about those things (that played upon my senses), I think particularly about the rivalries we had in the AFC West with the Chargers and Raiders and Broncos and Chiefs. I think of something different as I think about playing each of those teams in their stadiums. When I think about playing the Raiders, for a lot of my career they were in L.A., and I remember the sound and a little bit of an intimidating feeling of just hearing your cleats click down that huge tunnel that leads on to the Coliseum floor. Both locker rooms emptied into the same tunnel and I just remember particularly that walk from the locker room out on to the Coliseum playing floor, particularly when we played the Raiders there in the AFC championship game in 1983—the year they actually won the Super Bowl, beating the Redskins. And Al Davis had painted the entire wall (at the Coliseum) that you face as you come out into the tunnel black and put the Raider logo in the center of that wall.

I remember going out on the field and watching The Pointer Sisters sing the national anthem, all dressed in black sequined dresses.

"When I think about the Broncos, I think about Mile High Stadium which was always the most difficult place to win, and yet the most gratifying when you did or were fortunate enough to beat the Broncos. To beat the Broncos in Mile High Stadium was a great accomplishment, they had great fans. I remember the way they had it arranged. There was a small fence that was right behind the bench on the visitors' side. They would put the most obnoxious fans right behind that fence and they'd be barking at you the whole game.

"I can remember coming out of the locker room at Mile High Stadium and just the smell of the grass and the lack of oxygen that took you a quarter or a half to sort of adjust to. Playing a game with shortness of breath in front of 80,000 screaming fans, some of them dressed in nothing more than a Denver Bronco barrel.

"The high crown at Arrowhead (Stadium in Kansas City) seemed like it dropped two feet. It seemed like you were running downhill as you were running toward the sideline.

"The Chargers' (stadium) was a great field to play, because you were guaranteed to be playing on grass and it was always going to be sunny when you played in San Diego, which coming from Seattle was something we always looked forward to. The one thing about playing the Chargers I remember was the sight of so many sailors attending the Chargers' games. They'd be out there in their white and navy uniforms, it was just kind of an unusual sight. They'd always have a lot of sailors at the game and inevitably they were drinking and inevitably there were fights that would break out in the stadium.

"The Chargers were always a fun team for me to go play against because it was just fun to watch Dan Fouts and Kellen Winslow and John Jefferson and Wes Chandler and Charlie Joiner. Just being a receiver it was always fun to watch their passing game, because they would make incredible catches and Dan Fouts was just one of the best passers in NFL history. We knew our offense was going to be on the field a lot that game because ... they would move the ball so quickly up and down the field that we'd be back on the field before you knew it.

"The smell of the liniment as you walk through the training room and the whirr of the whirlpools that were inevitably working in the locker rooms. And the ceaseless noise of people extracting ice from the ice machine to heal their wounds from the previous game.

"What a great feeling it was to wake up totally beat up and sore like you've just been in a car wreck on a Monday morning after you've won the game on a Sunday afternoon. It's a great feeling. It really is. You know you've been out there and you've been in the battle and you were victorious. As painful as it was, it was very gratifying to wake up and know that those sore muscles and the turf burns and the swollen joints were all accepted as part of the price for the victory that you won on the previous Sunday. And it really made it all worthwhile. You'd win a game on Sunday and you couldn't wait to play the next week. You'd lose a game on Sunday and you couldn't wait to redeem yourself on the following Sunday. That's the way it is in the NFL, you live from Sunday to Sunday, but always anxious to play the next game.

"All those memories, it's sort of like a drug addict that has a flashback from an LSD trip or something. I have those flashbacks when I walk into a stadium. When I attend a large event with a big crowd, you just kind of hear the murmuring of the crowd before the game or in between plays, all those sort of things trigger a lot of these memories. I can walk into a stadium now, whether it's a baseball game or my son's football game and my palms will start sweating just because you have these flashbacks. They are great memories. They really are.

"I had a chance to speak at the chapel service before the University of Oklahoma played Texas Tech down in Norman. Coach (Bob) Stoops, who was in the chapel service, heard me speak and came up and introduced himself and just was saying, 'Thanks for coming, we really appreciate it, enjoy the game ...,' that type of thing. And then at the end, he said something like 'Good luck to you. If there's anything I can do to help you, let me know.' And then he pats me on the butt. And I thought 'You know, I haven't been patted on the butt in a long time, but it was such a typical coach or football sort of thing to do.' When you would do that you wouldn't even think about it, but when you hadn't been in that arena for a long time it just was pretty funny.

There I was in my jeans and a T-shirt getting ready to go to the game after speaking in the chapel service when the coach pats me on the butt to wish me well. That was like a reminder of some of the unique aspects of being in that arena."

CHAPTER 4

Camaraderie

Camaraderie

There is a kinship among athletes, similar to the brotherhood of firefighters or the thin blue line that connects policemen. They have families at home, but their teammates and co-workers are another family. They are together both at the office and on the road for weeks and months under unique and tense conditions. They can relate to each other in a way they feel we can't understand, because we are not in this family.

Before, during and after games or practices, players just enjoy being around other players. And now they talk about their passion for that camaraderie.

Welcome to the fraternity …

Camaraderie

Texas forward Chris Owens

"The biggest thing I like now is the camaraderie with my teammates. Playing on the road is tough, but road trips are fun. I like getting on the bus, the plane ride. I like the conversations we have at dinner or late at night when we're unwinding. We talk some about the game, but mostly we are always making jokes with each other. Guys like (guard) Royal Ivey are always joking. Being able to connect with my teammates is special. We're all so different, but we have to learn how to blend just so we can try and get the job done."

St. Joseph's point guard Jameer Nelson

"Where I come from, it's like a basketball town. In order for me to stay out of trouble, I had to do something. I played basketball and baseball, but I stuck with basketball. It fit with my lifestyle. I like the traveling, being around my team. You don't have to become friends with your teammates, but I like to become friends with all my teammates.

"Some people are selfish and they trust themselves more than they trust their teammates. I always want to be the person who takes the last shot, but I know there's somebody on the team that can do the same thing. If I was out there not enjoying my teammates, or having no confidence in them, I'd almost be playing myself. And that's not possible. It's hard doing one-on-five."

Connecticut basketball coach Jim Calhoun

"More and more, guys I'm around who have played a lot of basketball or coached a lot of basketball, been involved in the game, I ask guys when they stop coaching, for example, 'What they miss most?' and they say, 'Not having a team.' They need a team to belong to. To feel the great feeling of success and the dagger of defeat. I think those things are very important for a lot of our lives."

Former Northwestern running back Damien Anderson

"It's a combination of it all. A big run, knowing what's going to go on before it happens. Being a student of the game and the camaraderie with teammates. You go in strangers and some teammates end up being closer than family members. They know more about you. They are with you in adverse situations. I call them my family.

"I like riding back on the bus after games. You talk to other players at other positions and learn what they go through. It's an outpouring of thoughts. When you respect each other, you talk about certain things."

Washington Wizards shooting guard Richard Hamilton

"Just being out there and being part of a team. Just being part of an atmosphere where everybody loves to play basketball. I think when you're out on the floor and you're just running up and down the floor and you're tired, and you hit a game-winning shot, this is the reason why I love the game."

Former NBA player Austin Carr

"The thing I enjoyed was when your peers acknowledged you. I loved it when they told me I did good."

Golden State Warriors forward Antawn Jamison

"I love every aspect about the game of basketball. ... The camaraderie of 12 or 13 guys on the team, four coaches and when you are out there on the court, just five against five. You are pushing and shoving and doing whatever takes to win and whatever it takes to be successful.

"The relationship that grows during the weeks and months you are with the guys on your team, and trying to get all on one page and then out there on the basketball court."

Minnesota Twins infielder Denny Hocking

"The camaraderie, spending eight months with the same group of guys. The guys in this clubhouse are great. When you're losing, everyone is trying to pick everyone else up. We've had guys that have played in the minor leagues together, and now we're all here, rowing the boat in the same direction. I think that's why you see a lot of guys come to the park five hours before the first pitch, because they like hanging out together. I wish I could hang around longer after the game, but with kids, my wife wants me home."

Pittsburgh Pirates infielder Pokey Reese

"Just my teammates. Every year, I can't wait for spring training. During the offseason, it gets boring sitting around home. I can't wait to see my friends."

Tampa Bay Buccaneers safety John Lynch

"There's a lot of reasons (to love football). The ones that come to mind right off bat are the unbelievable sense of camaraderie. Bill Walsh used to tell us, 'What greater thing in the world than people from all different backgrounds, all different races, all different religions coming together. And you go out there on Sunday, and everyone's on the same team.' I think it's the purest game in the world. Every game is a challenge physically and mentally. It calls on you coming together as a unit and trusting your team-mates."

Baltimore Ravens coach Brian Billick

"Once you get away during the offseason, you miss the rela-tionship with the players and coaches. You hear people say that a lot when they retire, but I'll miss that when I'm out of the game."

New York Jets free safety Damien Robinson

"The friendships. A lot of times, you might hear about a guy and, when you get in the league, you get a chance to compete against him."

Pittsburgh Steelers strong safety Lee Flowers

"I think the ability to trust 21 other guys on the field. You put so much faith in the guy right next to you. In this day and age and the way society is it's hard to trust other people outside your immediate family. Just being able to get dressed, get undressed, take a shower with and eat dinner with and sleep in the same hotel with a grown man is very special. ... Just being able to trust another human being. It's definitely another family because if you think about it I spend more time with the guys in the locker room than I do with my own family. This day and age, professional sports is an all-year-round thing now, so for the years that you have an opportunity to play that's pretty much your family for that period of time and it's definitely your family away from home."

CBS broadcaster and former NFL player Craig James

"I think the beauty of football is that you look at you teammates in a huddle and you realize that that person who is standing next to you is depending on you. And, all 11 players have got to do their job, if you're going to be successful. It's the greatest team sport going, and it's a violent sport that is played with body control.

"It's one of those things that, I don't know when it was that I first realized it was a violent sport played with passion and body control, but at some point I remember feeling as if I was going to war and I had a handful of teammates in the huddle that were counting on each other and everybody had to do their job. It's a great feeling knowing that a play is successful because everybody did what he was supposed to do.

"Sometimes it's not saying anything, it's just looking at a guy. Or, it's a quarterback. The year we went to the Super Bowl, Steve Grogan in the huddle calling his own plays, which was rare, and Steve asking, 'Guys can we run this play? Can we run Red Right 34? Will it make it? We need 2 yards.' And that offensive line saying, 'Yes, we can get it done,' and then Steve saying, 'All right fellas, let's go: Red Right 34 on 2, ready, hut. Let's go.' To me that sense of teamwork and camaraderie is awesome and the belief in each other. To me, that's what I miss about it: the sheer drive and determination required to be successful."

Dallas Cowboys running back Emmitt Smith

"I make a lot of money, but I don't play the game for money. I play it because I love the competition and I love my teammates. You develop a passion for the game when you see each of your teammates working out in the offseason or practicing as hard as they can to achieve a common goal."

Pro Football Hall of Famer Jack Ham

"That's what makes this game so unique, it's not just you. You want to play well because you don't want to let a teammate down. I don't want to let down Joe Greene or L.C. Greenwood who plays in front of me. Make sure I do what I have to do, my responsibility. That's what I've felt about this game. That's why I love it so much because I can't equate it to any other sport.

"I would never want to let my teammates down. That's just the feeling we had on my football team."

St. Louis Rams offensive lineman Adam Timmerman

"Just going to the battle with your teammates, I think that's the best part. That's what makes it the most fun. You're going out there and you're laying it on the line for them as much as yourself. I think that's the fun part and that's what keeps it interesting, too. Just to create a whole new chemistry each year. Each team is different, you got a lot of the same guys, but just a lot of the camaraderie that's built every year.

"I'd say in high school and the start of college, when you come in with guys to your first year of college, those guys you came in with when you were freshmen, and started to build those relationships and as it grows and grows until you're juniors and seniors, I think that's where is really becomes something really cool, because those relationships having taken you four years to build and you all came in together and you've been building this thing—you're team—for all that length of time. I think that's when it was the coolest. It's hard to do at the pro level because of the personnel changes all the time. To a certain extent, I think it's the same because guys, even if you were on a different team, they're new to the team or whatever, you've kind of had similar experiences.

"I think the enjoyable part for me is a lot of the locker room stuff. The stuff that goes on in the locker room either pre practice or pre game or post game. A lot of things happen on the field that happen really fast, I think probably the most fun is rehashing certain plays with the old line sitting around, 'Hey do you remember on that one play where that guy came over to you, and you chipped him and we knocked him down on the ground.' You know, just kind of reliving them, because they kind of happen so fast during the game, but when you can sit around and talk about them, (it's fun). Of course, you think you're so much better than you really were, probably. But that's always the fun part of it.

"When that day comes that it's time to hang up the cleats, I think that's the part I'll miss the most."

NASCAR crew chief Frank Stoddard

"I'm not the kind of guy that likes to stand around. I like to be involved in something. I like to jump in and help the guys when I can.

"We took the engine out of the car we wrecked and put it in the backup car. They said it took 37 minutes on TV and that was cool. I've had a lot of guys that came up to me afterward and told me that would be the highlight of their career. That was neat. That felt like Saturday night short track racing. All your friends are hanging out helping you. They all had their guys over there helping us and nobody left until it was done. It was neat. That's what makes it fun. We'll sit around for 10 or 15 years and tell that story. When Robby and I are out there on the lake or when Jimmy and I are doing something, we will go back through the worst of times and say 'Well, it's not bad yet, do you remember the time when we had to change the motor from this car to that car?' That's what makes this fun. That's what makes life go round."

NASCAR driver Kyle Petty

"I grew up with it, I love to drive a race car. I love the competitiveness. But at the same time I love the people, whether it's the other drivers or the media, or people from the other teams. Just being around people who love the sport, who have the same passion for the sport, that are here because they love the sport.

"Sure, there's people here making money, but there's a lot of people that are here just because they love racing and they love race cars. I think that's what's exciting for me, is to be around that kind of attitude."

San Diego Chargers quarterback Doug Flutie

"I love being around the players, hanging out, talking and playing basketball. There's a common bond when you work hard together and earn each other's respect. There's a bond that you can't really explain unless you've been a part of it. ... I just love being on the field. I'm never in a hurry to come off the field. I'll hang around and drop kick field goals."

NASCAR owner Ray Evernham

"I've always raced as far back as I can remember. I haven't known anything else. It's always been my passion. I love the cars. I love the people. ... When you get to do the thing you've always wanted to do—that's pretty special.

"As tough as it gets sometimes, I just love being around the cars. Other than my family and my son, there is nothing else in my life that has ever interested me other than auto racing. I love the cars and I love the people.

"I don't know if it's the challenge of solving problems, of making cars go faster. I like that. But as far back as I can remember—even in kindergarten—I can remember drawing pictures of cars. As much as sometimes that I bitch like everybody else that I'm burned out, I have a very blessed life and to be able to do what I do, I feel honored."

Oakland Raiders fullback Jon Ritchie

"There are a lot of things that I don't notice when I'm out there, like the people and crowd and the pressure of the situation. It's like you're out there doing this thing that you've done for your whole life, the thing that you most enjoy, and now you're getting a chance to do it. It truly is a game that you've grown accustomed to, but there are constant permutations. You're always excited to see what's going to happen next.

"The discussions in the huddle, that's an interesting dynamic in itself. Of course, every guy has a personality that you've grown accustomed to in practices and meetings and spending time together hanging out off the field. When game day comes around it's always interesting to see the changeable nature of personality given the situation. There are some guys who are even-keel all the time and there are some guys who are ALWAYS fired up—regardless of what's going on.

"That's something that no one will ever know, that camaraderie when you're in the huddle when everyone is kind of depending on one and another. That's kind of the place where you regroup, go out for a short battle, six seconds for a play, pick yourself up off the ground, help your teammate up off the ground, go back and regroup in this huddle where you do have a chance to pick each other up emotionally before you have to go out there and do battle again. And there is that communication where you are laying out the plan for the battle and it's all so quick, but at the same time it can be very meaningful. The level of communication in that huddle between a quarterback and the team, between the offensive linemen amongst themselves and the wide receivers amongst themselves and between the running backs and one person to the next regardless of the position, giving each other a boost. A lot of times it's the forgotten realm of the playing field. If you think about it there's a lot more time spent in the huddle during the game than there is actually playing. That's why the games last three hours when there's only 60 minutes of actual playing time.

"That's the part of the game that people never see and it is kind of interesting. A lot of times those seconds in the huddle can mean the difference between a successful play, a successful series and successful drive and winning and losing."

NASCAR driver Sterling Marlin

"I always enjoyed working on cars, being with my dad and racing. I can't remember a day since I was 12 that I haven't thought of a racecar. Once I got to drive one, I said, 'Gee, this is fun,' and I've been fortunate to get some breaks and make it in Winston Cup racing. Just being here and seeing everybody is a thrill."

Reds radio broadcaster and former baseball player Joe Nuxhall

"The biggest thing I love about the game is the clubhouse. Nobody realizes how much time you spend there. I've always just liked the feeling of walking into a ballpark."

New York Jets coach Herman Edwards

"(The game) brings a lot of people together for a common cause. It crosses all nationalities, religious beliefs, political beliefs. You have to put those things aside and come together for a common cause. The greatest thing about football is when the players hold hands in the huddle. It's a way of bonding and that's what's unique about the game.

"Watching it as a child, and then, all of a sudden, you get to participate in it. The more you participate, the more you find out about yourself. That's what it's about, giving yourself to other guys. It's not about you anymore, it's about a team. It's what you can bring to the team and what you're able to do with a bunch of guys pulling together. As you get older, you enjoy it even more, because you understand the concept of team."

Pro Football Hall of Famer Steve Largent

"The camaraderie that you develop over the course of a season playing with your teammates. The thing that I think about, particularly now reflecting back on my career, is how football brought together so many guys with such diverse backgrounds, different ethnic groups and different socioeconomic backgrounds from all parts of the country, and football really became the vehicle to create a type of unity that few other things in our society can do.

"You think about the huddle in a football game and it functions unlike any other committee would ever function. You have one person who is calling the play. Everybody has clearly defined responsibilities and roles that they play. There's no argument or debate. You call the play. You break the huddle. There's a sense of unity even in the clapping hands as you break the huddle together. In that respect, it is really a very, very unique experience in our society and culture today. Those are some of the things that

I cherish."

CHAPTER 5

Competition

Competition

A pair of shortstops—one from the past and one from the present—are connected by a common love for their game.

Soon after his first-ballot election to baseball's Hall of Fame, Ozzie Smith spoke with reporters and captured the spirit succinctly as if it was just another grounder into the hole: "I never played this game to make it to the Hall of Fame. I played it because I loved it."

Boston Red Sox shortstop Nomar Garciaparra understands. He realized it most in late July of 2001, when he returned to the field after missing the first part of the season following wrist surgery. After that first game back on the grass in the shadow of Fenway's Green

Monster, he told reporters: "I definitely missed it.

"I love playing the game. It puts a smile on my face."

Competition

Former Minnesota Twins coach and baseball player Paul Molitor

"I loved the game specifically, other than the aesthetics and surroundings, because it's unique to me (more) than other professional team sports. It's more of a one-on-one confrontation, the battle between the pitcher and the batter, and the other players get involved after that confrontation takes place. ... There's the idiosyncrasies of the game that while people might know the game in terms of how to put together a batting order and when to bring in the closer, they might not know what middle infielder is going to cover second base according to what pitch is thrown and how the infielders might tip the corner infielders to off-speed pitches so they can cheat to the line. There's the communication and trying to pick up signs from second base, the little details that give players edges in games and give their clubs chances to win. It's a game that can go very deep in intellect, and I really enjoy that part of baseball."

Former Nebraska quarterback Eric Crouch

"The preparation is what makes the sport special to me. We prepare so hard, and we have that fight and competitive nature to want to be the best. After you've prepared and done everything you possibly could, the sweat, blood, discipline and time you've spent. And then going out and winning a game, knowing how hard it was. The satisfaction in that and the relief knowing you did it, you accomplished your goal."

NASCAR driver Dave Blaney

"When you get out there on your own, it's kind of like you against everybody. It's a war of wills to get everything you can get out of your car. If you can get everything out of yours, then maybe you can beat someone with an equal car that can't get everything out of theirs. There's a lot of that in taking pride in winning and taking pride in building a better car than anyone else's. There are certain things you do to prepare it and to work on it to make it the best. I think any racer can jump in a car and get to 90-percent real fast. It's that last 10 percent that separates the guys that win from the guys that don't."

Tennessee Titans offensive lineman Brad Hopkins

"It's the competitive spirit, most definitely. I think there are a lot of things that people do to blow off steam and dispense energy. When you do it in such a competitive nature it really doesn't matter what you're doing. It just happens to be a sport that creates that kind of passion when you're playing against people that you know are physically trying to get it done against you. So you're competing, you're working hard and you have to work with other people to have success. This is totally different than tennis or even basketball in most respects, because you're success totally depends on everybody, rather than just yourself. That competition level definitely makes a difference.

"You have to have a moderate amount of affection, if you will, to be able to put yourself through these grueling tasks and risking physical harm. You have to be able to take care of that stuff. As far as family members it's not on that scale."

Minnesota Twins bullpen coach Rick Stelmaszek

"I still like going to the ballpark, I still like going to work. It's not a chore, it's fun. Every day is different. It's hard to explain. The competitive juices, that's still what I like the best. You're playing against the best."

NASCAR crew chief Frank Stoddard

"I believe that I am one of the most competitive people in the world. I will do whatever it takes to win. If I have to get under someone's skin in a golf game to throw them off the tee, whatever it is. I thrive on competition. I like the element of competition. I don't play anything as hard unless I have somebody to compete beside—and then I'll beat them. I'll try to beat them and if I can't, I will try to convince them that I've beat them before I'm done."

Former Oklahoma linebacker Rocky Calmus

"You can do things you can't do out in public or you'd get arrested. You can hit a guy as hard as you want. You can blindside him. They might call you cheap, but it's all right. A guy is coming across the middle and he's not looking, and you can just deck him. Just lay him out. You're always challenged, and I like a good challenge. ... Batted down ball, tackle for loss, interception, making big plays. I always have been on great teams. I enjoy knowing people can't move the ball on you."

NASCAR driver Ricky Rudd

"As a young kid competing against other competition, you try to do your best and for me that was racing cars. I was running Winston Cup cars when I was 18. There wasn't a lot of jobs in between that. I like flying. I'm a pilot. If I had another choice I may have tried flying—being just a pilot would not have satisfied me, I would have probably had to be a military combat pilot to get the same kind of adrenaline rush."

NFL linebacker Shawn Barber

"What I love is the competition. Whether it's football or any other sport or any other event, playing darts or checkers, people who know me know I love to compete. And in anything where you can win or lose, I'm avid about winning.

"Football allows you to compete in about 60 individual competitions within every game. You have so many one-on-one battles, with the quarterback, the running backs, receivers and linemen. You're constantly being challenged physically, as well as mentally with different sets, formations and trick plays. You are faced with so many different things where you have to think fast and react to compete and succeed.

"The physical nature of the game is something I love. It's the only sport that allows you to be this physical on so many occasions. Everyone knows the saying, 'Football allows you to do things on the field that if you did them off the field, you would be in jail.'

"Everyone loves playing the games. But what drives me is the love of competing, even in practice. Every day that you go out there, you have a chance to make plays, during the inside running drills, in the seven-on-seven passing drills, in everything."

NASCAR driver Terry Labonte

"What drives you is wanting to win that next race, wanting to win that next championship. Knowing that if we can get it right, we can still do this ... wanting to be successful. That's what drives me.

"Back when the rumors came out that I was going to retire, I told someone, 'I'm not ready to retire. I may get pissed off and quit, but I'm not going to retire anytime soon.' I really want to win one more title so I can win in three different decades."

NASCAR driver Elliott Sadler

"I think it's the competition. I just think it's cool to be able to race—the adrenaline, the side-by-side, the bumper-to-bumper. It's just what I loved as a kid. It's what was bred into me. My brother raced. My cousins raced. My father and my uncles raced. I guess it's just the sport itself. Everything it offers both on and off the track, the speed and the action. It's not just 500 miles running in circles, every lap you are racing against somebody. You're never really by yourself and that's what I love about it."

NASCAR driver Jeff Green

"All of us have competitive juices that we have to exhale from time to time. The love of being able to drive a race car as fast as you can drive it quenches the need for speed. Being able to make a living from something I love and enjoy doing when 90-percent of us would do this for nothing. ... There's nothing better than being in a race car and getting the most out of it."

NASCAR driver Kevin Harvick

"Everything is going good when you work with guys who want

to win as bad as you do. That makes it fun and we have a whole lot of fun at racing. I thrive on the competition and that's what keeps me here. It's what I've wanted to do ever since I was a kid."

NASCAR driver Sterling Marlin

"When the car is really running good and you feel like you have a chance of winning—that's cool. The past couple of years I still like being here, but I had more of a feeling that we would be happy finishing 10th. Now we come, and I feel like we have a chance at winning and that makes my outlook a little better."

Illinois point guard Frank Williams

"It's the competition. That's what's so thrilling about it. You always have someone who can play at a higher level, and you try to match their intensity and their level and you try to compete. You can always determine which guys you need to step up for by the way the game is going. It's an energy inside of you."

Syracuse forward Preston Shumpert

"It's kind of hard to put it in words, but it's the desire to want to play and compete in a sport you love so much and are willing to sacrifice a lot for. I enjoy playing and being able to do well.

"Basketball is as much mental as it is physical. ... I love playing against different people. The more people you can play against, the more confident you can be in your game. You've got to feel confident in yourself and your ability to do well. My first year in college, Richard Hamilton was the first person I played against that really showed how much work I had to do. The fact that he's in The League (NBA) showed how much of a player he was. If I was at the point then that I am now, I feel like I could have played with him."

Charlotte Hornets forward P.J. Brown

"I just love the competition. I love just going out and competing. The game is just a lot of fun, and the thrill of victory, to work so hard in practice and then to put it all together and come together as one in a game, that's a great feeling.

"The battle, just coming out and battling, and the preparation, coming out and working hard to be the best I can. I love the game within the game. People think you just go out there and play, but the mental games you play with each other really are a game within the game. You've got to size a guy up, you've got to scout them, analyze them, see what his strengths and weaknesses are, compare them to what my strengths and weaknesses are, look at how they fit into the team's overall strengths and weaknesses. It's exciting to me to try to figure out the key to the other team, the pieces to their puzzle, and then to try to go out and beat them."

Hall of Fame basketball player Bob Cousy

"It wasn't just that I choose basketball specifically. I love the competition. If it had been baseball or football, I would have loved that just as much. It's just that my skills and my physical assets were obviously better geared to basketball."

Indiana Pacers guard/forward Ron Artest

"What I like most about basketball is playing against the best players in the world and playing before big crowds and playing on television. But as for the game itself, I guess I like getting steals more than anything. When I was a kid, I used to get in trouble for going into stores and stealing things. But I got away with it a lot. And now they pay me to do it. I love stealing the basketball from another player and then dribbling down the court for an easy basket."

Houston Rockets point guard Steve Francis

"I think just the challenge of competing against guys who are the best players in the world, whether it's the NBA level, high school or college. I think that the challenge, something that really pushes me is to be able to do different things on the court knowing that the other guys are just as good and able to do the same thing."

Washington Wizards shooting guard Richard Hamilton

"The competitiveness. Anytime you can compete and one person wins and one person loses, that's the thing you got to love, competing each and every night in everything you do."

New Jersey Nets coach and former NBA player Byron Scott

"I think the one thing that made me think the NBA was great was the rivalry we had with the Celtics. There was such great tension between the teams, and hatred, but respect, too. I had never seen anything like that. I guess I saw it in high school, but this was just on a different plateau. It was so neat to have a team playing on the other coast that you always looked at to see what they were doing. When we beat them in their building, that was the best feeling in the world."

Golden State Warriors forward Antawn Jamison

"I love every aspect about the game of basketball. Getting up early in the morning, practicing every day, coming home and your back is sore and your joints are just killing you. As far as the game situation, just to hear thousands of fans to cheer with you or against you."

Former baseball/football player Deion Sanders

"The one-on-one challenge. It's similar to the challenge of being onc on one as a cornerback. It's one on one with the pitchers. I'm trying to get him, he's trying to get me. … Man against man, that's self explanatory, my brother. Athlete against athlete. You can't blame anybody but yourself."

Former President and Michigan offensive lineman Gerald Ford

"I primarily loved the game because it was a team effort. There was a competition first to make the team then to compete statewide. Competition has always been an import part of my life.

"I like to look at the (offensive) line play because that's what I played. Most people keep their focus on the man with the ball, but those of us who played line like to see a good block."

Toronto Blue Jays pitcher Dan Plesac

"It's a cat-and-mouse game (when pitching against Paul O'Neill). He knows he's probably going to get one good pitch to hit during an at-bat, he's trying to work the count to get that pitch, and I know he's doing it, and it's all about who can get the upper hand first. Same thing with (Rafael) Palmeiro, Mo Vaughn, Barry Bonds, Mark Grace, Tony Gwynn. They know what I have, and I know what they are looking to do. The situation of the game might dictate the way I pitch Paul O'Neill Monday as opposed to Tuesday. I might be more aggressive with my fastball or in a close game, might go to my breaking ball more. There are times when (O'Neill) has had good swings off me, where he's had good swings off me when I thought I had him in the count, or a pitch I thought was the right one, and he'll foul it back, and I can read he was sitting on it, he got it, and didn't put it in play. And there are times when I've made a good pitch to a guy like O'Neill, but he's such a good hitter, he'll foul it off or hit it down the line. That's the cat-and-mouse game. You try not to fall into a pattern, and it's difficult to do. You go from pitch to pitch trying to read the way he took a pitch, or the way he swung at a particular ball."

Wisconsin quarterback Brooks Bollinger

"The thing that separates football from other sports and makes it special is the fact you only play a limited number of games. You do stuff all year long, spring, fall camp, lifting, and you put so much into preparing for each game. It's so emotional. One or two losses is a big deal. In other sports, you can afford to drop a couple. The emotion that is involved in that is unbelievable and intensifies it."

Philadelphia Phillies outfielder Doug Glanville

"The one thing that stays consistent is the competition, the challenge to be the best you can be amongst the best. It's like a test; it really tests you to see intestinal fortitude. It's a great lesson in life. I don't think baseball is that different. Any time you do something every day, you see ups and downs from everybody."

New York Mets pitcher Al Leiter

"What I love the most about the game, especially at this point in my life and this stage in my career, is the true essence of competing. The fun of being in a major league stadium on a major league mound trying to get a major league hitter out at this level. And knowing the art and expertise and the talent to get the hitter out. I love to compete. It's the competition that drives me."

Former baseball player Willie Horton

"Staring down a pitcher. It's just me against him. I still miss that. It's one on one; nobody else. It's a great test of patience, of courage, of strength. There is such mutual respect there because both people know what kind of damage the other one can do."

Houston Astros second baseman Craig Biggio

"You never really know what is going to happen on a baseball field. Just when you think you've seen it all, you'll see something else happen that you've never seen before. It's such a great game because it fluctuates day to day.

"Baseball is a game where a guy is throwing a round object and you hit it with a round bat, hopefully in a direction that they can't catch it. It's the only sport where you don't control the offense."

Tampa Bay Devil Rays catcher John Flaherty

"Baseball players are competitors and that's what motivates me, the competing. Competing against the other team, competing against the pitcher, competing against the other team's lineup, all those things that get your competitive juices flowing, and in professional baseball you're competing for your career every day. To me it's not really a sound or a smell that makes me love the game, it's the competitive aspect of it."

U.S. Congressman and former college football player J.C. Watts

"I think I owe a lot of my competitive juices to being able to operate in the arena of competition by way of football.

"The thing that kind of got my juices going is when coach (Barry) Switzer was hired as the Dallas coach. I had started kind of paying attention again and then I was invited down to a Cowboys' game. I was on the sidelines, I was there on the field and I saw these guys running out and that was the first time in seven or eight years that I said, and that I actually felt, 'God, I miss this.' Even today I'm over the playing part, obviously, but I watch it and I go to OU games and I'll see the Cowboys play a couple times a year and saw the Redskins play, and I think I am to the point now where I don't want to play, but I am to the point where I say, 'God, I'd like to be doing something to compete.' Something where you go out and physically challenge yourself to win, you have to do something physical and to combine the physical and the mental talents to compete in some arena."

Auto racing legend Mario Andretti

"Racing captured my imagination when I was just a young teenager. And the feeling kept getting stronger and stronger. I guess all the challenges of every day, the competition, the pride of accomplishment and all the satisfaction you can derive from winning—that's what kept me motivated. That's what kept me going from year to year and luckily I was able to go for a pretty long career. But it came from a total passion for my work.

"I really had a special respect for versatile drivers such as (A.J.) Foyt, Dan Gurney, people like that who could win at different disciplines. And I had the opportunity to move around and drive for really good teams even though it may have been on a part-time basis because my main effort was always single seaters. Then if you could win in someone else's sandbox, that was extra special.

"But I was pretty ambitious in my day. I didn't have any time off, but I didn't want any time off. If I saw a hole in the schedule, I would plug it up with another race somewhere. That's what I lived and breathed for."

Former NFL player Jessie Tuggle

"I love the game. First of all, to compete week in and week out, to go out there and show people you are the best in the world at what you do. All the guys you compete against, they're the best in the world at what you do. You go out there and play against a Pro Bowler or a potential Hall of Fame running back or anybody like that, you want to go out and play your best and it brings the best out of you."

New York Jets coach Herman Edwards

"The one thing I love about the game is the competition, going on the road and winning a game where a lot of people think you can't win. You never win the game on paper, and that's what's great about football. A game is like a bunch of different little battles. Every player has a battle that Sunday. If you win the little battles, you win the war, you win the game."

Indianapolis Colts quarterback Peyton Manning

"For me, it's not just about the game, I mean I love practice. A lot of guys don't. Offensive lineman don't and I understand that, but I'm a quarterback and practice is not as hard on my body as it is for offensive lineman. I like going to practice. I like going to work on a Wednesday, getting a game plan, trying to put it in the works on Wednesday, Thursday, Friday and Saturday and then taking the game plan and putting it to work on Sunday."

Detroit Lions CEO and president and former NFL player and broadcaster Matt Millen

"My passion has increased with my increase in the understanding of the game. At its elementary level, I love the elementary things of the game, which of course were the physical part of it and a chance to be aggressive and then as I grew in my understanding of the game I understood schematically that part of the game of how you use personnel and how your personnel can be utilized in your respective scheme. And then as I grew more I got to really appreciate and love the chess side of football: If you do that, I do this. I can run certain defenses against your offense and eliminate part of your offense and make you have to find my weakness and play to my weakness and then take the strength of a player and use that. It's a very complicated game, and I have always likened it to a game of chess, which is a game that I love to play, it's just that the chess pieces in football, you have your pons and rooks and all those things, except in this game the pieces think for themselves, and that's what makes it so unique. There is still the factor that you don't know how the person will react. That's what I love about the game. I mean I love that part. There is no substitute for it anywhere else. You still have, it's inclusive at all those levels, down to the basics of the aggression to the physical to the schematic and the individual piece. I just think it's a fascinating game.

"The other part of this game that is not talked about, which is a part that I realized when I was in college that I really enjoyed, and that is personnel. I enjoy breaking a person down on film. If I didn't do this job and I wasn't in television, I would still do it. I would do it on a high-school level or I would do it someplace, because within each individual there are strengths and weaknesses, and they're being taught to play to their strengths and we are teaching to attack the weakness, and that's the fun part.

"So within each scheme and within all that stuff there is the complexities of each individual and you have to be able to identify them, and once they're identified you can start attacking the weak links. That, I just love that stuff. I have tapes right here on my desk of our own people I go through meticulously, see what a guy can and can't do and I think that's fascinating.

"It's just like a scientist would be in breaking down any molecular structure. Anybody who is looking for a code and anybody who is into just breaking things to their basic elements, regardless of your line of work. It's just finding the basic element, identifying it and then working it through. And once it's identified and once it can be applied, then you have something. I get excited about that every day. Everyday I walk in here and I throw a tape on and I look at something and I can see—Bing!—the guy doesn't have good feet. He can be beat here. Or, he's not good enough here, but he is strong here. We can use that. All those little things, I just enjoy them.

"I'm going to sound like a philosopher here, but all of life's complexities and—boy, I don't know how to put it, but—all life's little quirks are all embodied in this game, you see them all the time. From personality traits to physical things to basic things. For example, why does terrorism work in our world? Because people are afraid to be hurt. People have a fear of being hurt or injured or they let things get to their mind. You take that very same principal and apply it in football and it works. People don't physically want to be beat. So, when you can do that, it can become intimidating and you use it. There's all kinds of parallels.

"Ultimately, you know what it comes down to? It all comes down to this, that ultimately this is a people game and it still comes down to inter-personal skills and dealing with people on an individual basis, with their individual skills, and utilizing them or not utilizing them. Then also knowing the other part of it, the psychological part that plays in every business, also is applied here in football. It's the same thing, except here we have immediate results. I don't have to wait for a five-year forecast. I don't have to wait to see if a plan is implemented properly. I can see on Sunday if it worked or not.

"I've said this before and I'll say it again: That this game is just a microcosm of life itself. In any walk of life, it doesn't matter, change the title, it all exists. And all these things are there to be learned if you're willing to learn them and if you're willing to just take the time to be aware. They're all there."

Former NFL player Andy Russell

"I think the true love of the game or passion for the game was to challenge my athletic ability against the best players in the world—to go out and see if I could defeat their blocks or stop a play that they had designed to beat us. That was to me what I think I love most about football."

St. Louis Rams wide receiver Torry Holt

"The money is significant and great and it fuels guys. I was always a firm believer that if you love the game and had a passion for the game and what you do, the money would take care of itself. If you love what you do you're going to do the necessary things that keep your body in shape so that you can perform in training camp, minicamp and on Sundays. Passion and love comes before the money and anything else.

"I really love going out there and training and getting ready and playing against the Sam Madisons and the Ty Laws and the other great cornerbacks. I really love that."

Baseball Hall of Famer and Kansas City Royals vice president of baseball operations George Brett

"Everyday was a challenge to go out there and do something special and try to help your team win. I think deep down inside I'm a very competitive person and I don't think there is any game as competitive as baseball because you have one-on-one matchups four or five times a day—you against the pitcher. Someone is going to win and someone is going to lose. It's not like that in basketball where you can pass off the shot to somebody else. You're destined to be up in that batter's box and lot of times the game is on the line and you're facing their best pitcher and that's the ultimate challenge. You know some days you're going to win and some days you're going to lose, but those days you win you cherish forever.

"Every time I go to a game, there isn't a time that I don't want to go out and play. I go to minor league games and visit with our minor leaguers and put on a uniform and throw batting practice and hit fungoes to this day. I always get a chance to speak to the whole team and a chance to speak to the hitters and relay my experiences as a player.

"These guys (in a rookie league) were putting on a uniform for the first time in their professional baseball careers. I tell them,

'Give it your all and have as much fun as you possibly can, get as dirty as you possibly can.'

"I'm at a baseball game right now, I'm watching us beat the Tigers 4-1 in the top of the seventh inning. And, you don't think I would love to be 32 years old again and jump down there and play third base right now? Of course I would. But unfortunately Father Time crept up on me and at age 40 I had to retire. That was eight years ago, I'm 48 years old now but I still have a burning desire to go out there and play. My desire never left me—to be good and to be the player. What happened is my body kind of said, 'You know, this is enough. You've had enough of this.'"

Philadelphia Flyers right winger Rick Tocchet

"It's one of those few sports where you have to have a little bit of everything. You have to have some talent , but you also have to have a competitive edge and a grittiness to the game. You got to have a little bit of everything if you want to play this game. You can't just be one thing. You have to expect you are going to get hit or you're going to have to make a nice play, and not too many sports have that."

CHAPTER 6

Adulation

Adulation

Athletes are entertainers, providing joy to an audience by performing a sport. The crowd comes to the arena, the viewers click on televisions and the listeners tune in the radios to experience an athletic performance.

And for many of the athletes, the crowd is why they perform. The euphoria of giving the home fans a reason to cheer. The sweet accomplishment of denying the fans in another town. They enjoy the give-and-take relationship of pleasing an audience and feeling the crowd respond to their performance.

For some athletes, excessive fame is a hideous curse and bothersome burden. But for most athletes, it is a sweet reward to be admired by other people, recognized in public and asked by children: "Can you sign this?"

Adulation

Houston Rockets point guard Steve Francis

"The crowd, the arenas, whether you are home or on the road, there is always going to be a lot of people at the games. There is always going to be that one kid, you can tell if you look in the stands, you can see that one kid thinking about when he gets to the basketball court tomorrow he's going to try doing that certain move that Steve Francis or another player did. I think that is something that makes you feel the love and passion for playing."

Stanford guard/forward Casey Jacobsen

"This might sound corny, but I really believe that it is the moments when little boys and girls ask me for an autograph. This simple act reminds me of why basketball is so special to me. It connects me with people that I would never interact with if I didn't play basketball. I remember when I was young—I'm still a kid, but stay with me—how cool the college players were. I wanted to be like them and play like them. Now that I am one, I don't want to forget what it is like to be a child with dreams."

Former Nebraska quarterback Eric Crouch

"I'm a leader out there. And to feel like you are leading a team, helping guys out and people are looking to you for accountability and credibility and to be a leader makes you feel that much better. It's that sense of people needing you and wanting you to be there. To look up into the stands and see 80,000 people staring down at you, supporting you. And those are just the people who can get into the game—many more can't get tickets. You develop a name for yourself and also develop character."

Texas forward Chris Owens

"Playing in front of a big crowd is fun. There are a lot of emotions. At home, people are rooting for you, screaming for you. It's still good to be pretty nervous before a game. My favorite thing on the basketball court is dunking. When I go up for a dunk, the thing that's going through my head is I want to dunk the ball as hard as I can so I can raise the intensity of my teammates and the crowd."

Milwaukee Bucks shooting guard Ray Allen

"It's about being able to create electricity in a building based on something I do. For the fans to stand on their feet, you crave that applause. You look for respect from your opponents and claps from the fans. To go out there on the court and get people on their feet is the ultimate satisfaction. Whether it's a shot, a pass or going sky high for a rebound, it's making somebody go, 'Wow!' That's awesome."

Dallas Mavericks forward Eduardo Najera

"Basketball also helped me make friends and got girls to notice me, especially when I moved to the U.S. (from Mexico to San Antonio)."

Chicago Bulls guard Fred Hoiberg

"It's great being an NBA player when you're out at the store and some little kid comes up and asks you about the game and you're able to sign an autograph and give the kid a smile. It's also fun being with your kids a lot and being admired by others."

Orlando Magic point guard Darrell Armstrong

"The challenge gets you up and makes you love the game. When you get those stops or make a big basket, the roar of the crowd it makes you love the game. … Plus, the crowd is fun when it's against you on the road. Sometimes, the whole city is against you. You can be in a restaurant and a fan will run up to you and say 'We're going to get you tonight.' It's like they're playing against you, too. You go back to your hotel room, and you can't wait to get out there and play."

Golden State Warriors forward Antawn Jamison

"Of course, you love the millions of people that are watching on TV … Any close game, the ball is in your hand, the people are waiting for you to come through. And knowing that when you have the ball in your hand you are the best guy for the job. You know it's a close ball game, so something needs to happen and it's in your hand to make something happen, to make the people jump up out of their seats, to make the people have something to talk about the next day. For them to remember what you did and how you did it, those are the things that you remember on the court. ... When they need for that basketball to go into the goal and you are able to do that, just the reaction of the fans when that happens."

Colorado Avalanche center Chris Drury

"Big-play player? A lot of people say that about me—and I think it began when I was playing in the Little League World Series against Taiwan in 1989 and pitching in front of 40,000 fans. That can be a little scary. But it made me feel like I wanted to be the center of attention. Hockey is much faster, but I still get that same center-of-attention feeling, whether I'm breaking in alone on goal or trying to make a hard hit. I guess, it's a passion I have developed for reacting whenever I get in a crucial situation."

Philadelphia Phillies outfielder Doug Glanville

"The crowd is definitely a big factor, when you get a big one and they're just going crazy. You definitely can get into it. It's like you're on stage. But you get used to that, and it's not as prevalent in your mind so you say, 'Oh, I can't wait to hear that crowd.' "

New York Mets pitcher Al Leiter

"The other day I was walking with some friends in Manhattan. A kid walked by, he had a Mets shirt, (number) 22, I thought it was just a generic Mets shirt. I turned around, it had 'Leiter' on it. I just walked by and here he is wearing my jersey. It's very, very, satisfying."

Tampa Bay Devil Rays catcher John Flaherty

"It's funny I'll watch a tape during the offseason and I'll get a hit and I'll see the crowd react and those are things you never realize during the season. I might wake up 10 years from now and think I should have enjoyed those things more than I did. You get so caught up in the game and competing you don't let yourself get caught up in the crowd or the cheering."

Seattle Seahawks defensive lineman John Randle

"It's when I go back down to Texas and people tell me, 'I can remember when you were just running around here.' I guess it's when my friends tell me that they're so proud of me for what I've accomplished. That and just being around the league and being here for so many years is another accomplishment that I love about it. It's just sometimes realizing how much I know about the game. You sit around in a restaurant and hear people talk and they just don't understand football. There's not too many things I've been good at, but I know football and I like to sit there and listen to people talk like they think they know it, but they don't really know it."

Former Colorado State defensive back Jason Gallimore

"My first tackle came in Mile High against CU. That was the most amazing thing. To grow up watching Colorado and to get out there in Mile High and to make a tackle on that field was an amazing feeling. To hear everybody and look around. Those types of things are what make football amazing to me."

Pittsburgh Steelers strong safety Lee Flowers

"Just the thrill of you showcasing your skills in front of 65-70,000 people. These people are paying $40 a ticket to come see you play and people are pretty much setting aside their whole Sundays just to see you play. It's just a thrill to know that you have some kind of talent that somebody is willing to pay $40 just to watch and that's a thrill to myself."

Indianapolis Colts quarterback Peyton Manning

"Well the crowd, obviously, when you're playing football, is something to appreciate. When I was in high school, a thousand people was a good crowd for our game and of course playing at Tennessee every single Saturday in Knoxville had 107,000 people. There is not better environment than football at the University of Tennessee.

"I was at the beach the other weekend and there was some people throwing a football around. This guy was throwing the football and I went up to him—I had a hat on and some sunglasses—and he's throwing the ball pretty well. I said, 'You got a pretty good arm there. Did you play?' He said, 'Yeah, I played in high school and at a small college.' As he's throwing the ball, you can tell he really misses the game. Here is something that I get to do for a living. I truly appreciate the opportunity to keep playing the game that so many guys played growing up."

Former NFL player Andy Russell

"I blotted the crowd out. I wasn't there. It wasn't a distraction. Was I able to do that really all the time? No. Sometimes you could feel the crowd's excitement. There were games where I felt the Steeler fans won the game. I said, 'If we don't beat these people, they're going to come out on the field and beat them for us.' It was wild. I can remember playing in college against Oklahoma down in the Snakepit, and they were one of the top teams in the country and we beat them. It was just wild. Either to play in front of a home crowd that was excited or to take an away crowd and just shut them down, that was fun."

CHAPTER 7

Something to Prove

Something to Prove

The best basketball player on earth and perhaps in the history of the game was cut from his high-school team. If that motivated Michael Jordan's desire to succeed on the basketball court, then the NBA owes Jordan's former coach a huge debt of gratitude.

So many of us, top athletes included, have been down the same road as Jordan. A slight or a negative in our past provokes a positive in our present or future.

The desire to validate through achievement after disappointment, and sometimes just a plain chip on the shoulder are often the driving forces behind every step of some athletes.

Something to Prove

San Antonio Spurs point guard Terry Porter

"I have been doing this a long time now. I don't think I am going to fool anybody, I mean, everybody knows what I can do and what I can't do. I can still play, my body feels good, so I am going to keep going out there. People will say to me sometimes, 'Why don't you retire and just, you know, play golf?' When I was younger, I had all kinds of reasons to play, I liked the money, I liked the fame and all that, but when you get to my age, that stuff kind of fades away. All those little things, like the competition and the feeling of making big shots, don't matter so much. Now it's just the ring. I have been very close but I don't have one. I hate that. I can't tell you how much I hate it. So the things that drove me when I was younger don't drive me anymore. I am very focused on a ring. When the season starts, and we have 82 games to go, and I am tired and I am thinking, 'Man, a whole season ...' And I think about playing all those games, trying to stay healthy, travelling, trying to get to the playoffs, it's hard. But then, I just think about that ring and getting one more shot at it and it's like, 'All right, let's play.'"

St. Louis Rams wide receiver Torry Holt

"I think what really motivated the most was when I was younger I was so small I wanted to get out there and prove a point. Just because I'm so small doesn't mean I can't play just as good as the guys that are bigger than I am. Then I found that I was pretty good at it and it has been just down hill since then."

NFL defensive end Michael McCrary

"I love this game because of the respect you get from your peers. ... I started loving this game when I first realized I could kick people's asses, and that started when I first started playing. I wouldn't play if I was getting my ass kicked. I can't imagine that. But that's what the NFL is good for, weeding out people who can't play and kick ass.

"I love hearing about how great a player is, then beating him and taking advantage of him. I like going home and then watching it on film. That's when I say, 'Wow, what a great game this is.'"

Orlando Magic point guard Darrell Armstrong

"I had a lot of stops and had to go through the minor leagues. You just try to improve the game, try to get confidence. I had to go through so many crazy things like getting coins thrown at you when you play overseas. And the way the fans act over there, it's unbelievable. They're allowed to smoke cigarettes during the game, and all kinds of stuff is going on. It's like there's a party going on when you're playing basketball. It's almost like the XFL. It was something that put a lot of things into my spirit and made me want to get better and get to the NBA. You want to get to where you can play in front of the best fans in the world and people appreciate the game and little kids appreciate the game and coaches appreciate the game."

NFL linebacker Shawn Barber

"When you succeed, it shows you deserve to be out there. I came to the NFL from a small school (Richmond), and four years after getting here, I'm still the same guy from that same small school, still out there trying to show I deserve to be in this league. How can you not love that?"

San Diego Chargers quarterback Doug Flutie

"I love the challenges. I love the competition—not just in football, but all sports. I love the fact that I can do something, that I can go out and prove everybody wrong. I love going out and using my skills to play the game. It's fun. I love running with the ball and making people miss.

"The challenge of the two-minute situation, being down by four points and needing a touchdown to win. You have to get the ball in the end zone and you have to be in control.

"When I come off the field and the players and coaches have that look, without saying anything, that I did something special."

Montreal Canadiens center Doug Gilmour

"They said I was too small, too skinny. When I played my first NHL game I weighed 140 pounds. The experts said I wouldn't last, that a strong wind might knock me over. Over the years, I think I ran into every heavyweight in the league at one time or another. … What I want to know is: Where are all of the skeptics who said I was too small and too skinny?"

New York Jets running back Curtis Martin

"I love preparing. I love working out when no one is here (at the team complex). I love the challenge. My goal is to be mentally tougher, have more stamina, have more focus. Whatever it takes to beat my opponent, to crush them."

Los Angeles Kings right winger Ziggy Palffy

"When I came to the NHL everyone told me I was too chubby and too this and too that. In reality, all I needed to do was learn to score a few goals to get the critics off my back.

"All I ever heard about was what a great goal-scorer Mike Bossy was for the Islanders. So, I asked the PR guy to get me some tapes of Bossy. I would watch it over and over, trying to pick up some of Bossy's habits. I watched his hands, his positioning before each shot. First, I began to score a little more in practice. Then, I got confidence and began scoring in games. Now, they don't tease me as much that I'm too chubby."

Oakland Raiders team executive and Pro Football Hall of Famer Jim Otto

"Well, I guess the reason that I love football so much and I still do is it was a tough man's game and it was a way to express myself and gain recognition. To be recognized as being tough. That's why I like football so much. I thought of that from the time I was a kid until the today, if I could be out on the field I'd be tougher than the next guy. ... Football is tough. You want to spell football: T-U-F-F. It's not for weak-hearted guys. It's a tough sport. If you want to get into something else, play with the girls."

Chicago Blackhawks right winger Steve Sullivan

"Do you know how often it hurts to hear someone say you're too small? Well, it happened in New Jersey and again in Toronto. Heck, the Maple Leafs just put me on waivers because they didn't think I could play at the NHL level. My first game with Chicago I remember one of the league's biggest defensemen nearly knocked me cold with a bodycheck along the board. To add insult to injury, he said, 'Go home and play with the kids in your neighborhood.' Since then I try to remember that comment every time I get the puck. Maybe the fear of being plastered again has made me faster, because instead of being too small I seem to get faster and better every year."

NFL defensive back Blaine Bishop

"I think it's the competitiveness in it and to be the best because you know you're out there with the best athletes. To strive to be the best and have the best team and win a Super Bowl and I think that's what drives me as well as trying to prove to people from day one that I can play in this game and play well."

Toronto Blue Jays pitcher Dan Plesac

"I have to do a lot more physically to get ready to play, but I enjoy it. Now I appreciate more what I have to do to get ready to pitch, because I don't want to play just to play.

"My arm feels better than five years ago. My stuff isn't as good as it was when I was with Milwaukee, but it's a challenge to figure out ways to make the stuff I have still successful. I can't pitch guys the same way, I get razzed at, but I take a lot of pride in what I do. I take a lot of pride in watching the game, watching the hitters, remembering what I threw a hitter last year, remembering what I threw a hitter last week."

Boston Red Sox pitcher Pedro Martinez

"The challenge. The difficulty. I would like someone to dare me to win. Someone who would say, 'No, you can't.' That's the type of challenge I want: 'No, you're not capable of doing it.' That's what I like. I don't know, I might be crazy."

Illinois point guard Frank Williams

"In eighth grade—that's when a lot of guys were older than me, tougher than me—that's when I decided that when I got older I wanted to be one of those who beat up on someone else."

Tennessee Titans wide receiver Kevin Dyson

"You know that saying, you don't know what you have until

it's gone, that's definitely true for me, being a professional athlete who missed the whole season (missed final 14 games of 2000 season due to knee injury). I missed every little bit of it, the locker room, the talking with the fellas, the going over the game plan, the competing, the getting ready before game time, the on-the-field competition, the talking trash—I miss everything. One thing, I will never take this game for granted again. Not being able to walk for almost two months, not being able to run for almost six months, I won't take a play off or a rep off, because I don't know when it's going to be my last play."

Former NFL player Jessie Tuggle

"Throughout my whole career, I've worked as hard as I can to be the best I can be. It's sort of funny, from the outside looking in, the average fan would think that it's money that motivates me. It's not. On Sundays, you don't think about that. You just think about being the best that you can be and going out there and playing as hard as you can possibly play. Overall that's what motivates me, the love of the game and the respect I have for the game. That's what I love the most, what I'm passionate about. It's been a dream come true for me. It's a privilege to play in this league."

Seattle Seahawks defensive lineman John Randle

"The physical challenge of going against guys that are 6-6, 6-7, 300-and-some pounds. And being able to beat those guys. Just beating those guys. Because I was picked on as a kid and it's almost like me still getting back at those bullies. And I just love it.

"To me, it's like they look at me like they think they should kick my butt. And I know that's what they're thinking. But once we get out on the field and we're going at it, they realize, 'Hey, wait a minute, this little guy is not about to just let me whup his butt.'

"It's not that I didn't get along with people, I was such a nerd. I still am a nerd. I just didn't really fit in with a lot of people and I used to get picked on a lot. Now, I guess it's revenge of the nerd."

Baseball Hall of Famer and Kansas City Royals vice president of baseball operations George Brett

"That's a game I used to play with myself on occasion, on hot

Sunday afternoon games on the artificial turf, when it was maybe 100 degrees in Kansas City but maybe 140 with the heat index on the turf. I would see all these other guys about the fifth inning slowing down running to their position or off the field. 'You know what, I'm going to beat everybody. I'm going to be the first one off. I'm going to make an impression with the fans here. Hey, look at these other guys how slow they're running, but then look at me and how fast I'm running and the effort that I'm putting into the game.' It was just a game to me and I always enjoyed games within the game. Little things like that just kept you going.

"Yeah, I guess you could say I'm passionate about it and will be until I die. It's a fun game for me to watch and it's a fun game for me to enjoy. It's a blast for me to go out and play in the backyard with my three (children). They're all boys and they all like to play baseball. When I get home from this game today, I can guarantee the first thing my kids will say is, 'Dad can we play catch?' And the first thing Dad's going to say is, 'Well, where are your gloves?' And if they say, 'I don't know,' I'm going to say, 'Well, you can't play without a glove, so you better go find them.' Sometimes it takes them an hour to find them because they leave them under trees and bushes and stuff like that. But, we will play and do play a lot and the one thing I'm proud of is that I get a chance to play a lot with my kids. Hopefully I teach them the passion and the love and the respect for the game of baseball."

CHAPTER 8

Success

Success

Women who suggest men have trouble expressing their emotions just don't watch enough sports.

If you want him to go dancing, ladies, then join him in the end zone after a touchdown.

Never seen him cry, well, wait till he retires after a Hall-of-Fame career of alternating between throwing touchdown passes and enduring concussions.

Need a hug from him? Score a game-winning goal or basket and wait for his sweaty, but enthusiastic embrace.

As for kissing, that's easy for a man. It's the first thing he does to a piece of championship silverware before extending it in his arms over his head.

The games elicit unusual emotional outbursts from normally the most masculine of creatures, especially when the final act in their passion play is victory, championship or glory.

Success

Milwaukee Bucks coach George Karl

"Sports allow you to do things no one can take away from you. I've talked to little kids about this, and I really believe it. You give the game of basketball a tremendous effort and it gives you something back. There's an honesty to it. Sometimes it's winning. Sometimes it's a championship. The game has an ability to lift you that makes me like to hang around."

Chicago Cubs right fielder Sammy Sosa

"This is the only thing that I know. You want to be the best you can be. You've got to work hard to be the best. And the only way you can be the best is because you love it. You want to be there. You want to be the man. It's your responsibility."

New Mexico basketball coach Fran Fraschilla

"I tell young coaches, don't get into this business unless it's in your blood. The passion for me has been a lifetime one. I don't think I've woken up in 30 years that I didn't say, 'What am I going to do today to help myself become a better coach?' It's not a job, it's a lifestyle.

"Road wins are the best. There's nothing like getting on the bus, going back to the airport or hotel, eating that Subway sandwich after just getting a win on the road. To me, coaching is all about getting your team to handle adversity. Being able to go on the road and win in a hostile environment, getting your team to believe that, even though (the other) team has won 17 in a row at home.

"Many times I've gone up to the locker room after a home game, and it's just relief. But after a road win, the giddiness is hard to quantify."

NASCAR owner Richard Childress

"The desire to win, the desire to be the best, that's what I love about racing. ... Once you've been there and had a taste of what it's like to be at the top, you always work hard to get back there. And it's always harder to stay there once you make it there. That always drives competitive people to always want to do better, to be better, to try to be the best. After putting all the hard work into it, the reward comes from sitting back on the mountain in the winter and saying, 'We did it.'"

NASCAR driver Ricky Rudd

"To me, the only part I enjoy about racing is when you're competitive and you have a chance to win an event. I enjoy it as much as anybody. I was telling (team owner) Robert (Yates) the other day, if we have a car like this every weekend, I'll pay him to drive instead of the other way around."

Tampa Bay Buccaneers safety John Lynch

"To me, there is nothing better—and I'm only talking about in athletics now—than just absolutely cleaning someone's clock. There's a lot of different names for them. Our defensive coordinator Monte Kiffin calls them slobber-knockers. I liken it to hitting a home run. A lot of hits, they hurt, but the purest hits, you don't feel a darn thing. They don't come every game. They're the ones, they come a couple every season."

NASCAR driver Mark Martin

"Forget participating, I only like winning. The opportunity to have a chance to win is a tremendous privilege. Forget about baseball where you have a 50-50 shot of winning. You get very little payoff in this sport, but after 25 years of 100-percent total dedication, (winning) is what it's all about. Wins are tough to come by. They don't happen every week. The best wins are the ones you don't expect—they are only a relief. They don't even feel good. It's more like, 'Whew, I'm glad we didn't throw that one away.' "

Indianapolis Colts quarterback Peyton Manning

"To me there is no better feeling than when you really bust your butt all week long, studying tape, working extra time in the weight room or on the practice field and then winning the game on Sunday. It truly is a great feeling."

Mississippi quarterback Eli Manning

"Throwing that perfect pass late in a tight game. It's a strange feeling that's hard to describe. It's what keeps you coming out there and wanting to win."

Dallas Cowboys running back Emmitt Smith

"Winning is the ultimate prize and it takes hard work to achieve it. But it's hard to win without having a passion for the game. You need that passion to make you play harder in the fourth quarter, when you're dead tired. You need that passion on fourth-and-1 from the goal line. You need that passion to workout in the offseason, when you'd rather be playing with your kids."

Pro Football Hall of Famer Jack Ham

"The number one thing that I like about football. You need to have the whole team buying into that team concept. The part I like the most about it is when the whole team kind of loses itself for one common goal to win a championship. There is not a better feeling for me, especially after a Super Bowl, that you are the best in the world at least for that year and how collectively the team was able to accomplish that."

St. Louis Rams offensive lineman Adam Timmerman

"There are certain moments during a game, when you have either a good series or it's been a good quarter or two, where the offense is really rolling and you just know at that point that you're going to win the game. I guess that's the realization of winning, there's always some point in the game where you have that feeling. And that's a great feeling."

Hall of Fame basketball player Bob Cousy

"My commitment and passion was directed at winning and losing, and being such a highly competitive person, and basketball was the tool that allowed me to exercise that. ... When you lose, the food doesn't taste as good, the sex isn't as good, because your complete focus is on basketball."

New York Jets running back Curtis Martin

"The reason I love football is not because of football. I don't love football for football. I actually had to be talked into playing football by my mother. My passion for the game comes from the different doors football opens for me. I enjoy playing, yet without the passion, I don't think I would prepare and put my heart into it the way I do. It's important that, whatever I do, I do it with all I have. The way football allows me to impact other people's lives—whether that be physically, emotionally, spiritually, financially, giving advice, whatever—that's what gives me my love for the game."

Los Angeles Lakers forward Rick Fox

"Now I know how hard walking away from it is going to be. After we won (the first championship), I spent the summer doing everything possible to get in better shape so I could get to that same point to have that same feeling. … Winning a championship, you can't compare that to anything."

Washington Wizards shooting guard Richard Hamilton

"Just the way people react about (a game-winning shot). The fans. When you're going to play, even if you're playing on the playground, if you got guys on your team that want to win and you hit game-winning shot, even if there is nobody around but you and your teammates, you get a thrill that you can take with you for the rest of the day."

Arizona Cardinals assistant coach and Pro Football Hall of Famer Joe Greene

"When it hits you, when it dawns on you that you are going to be in the Super Bowl. I don't know if winning the Super Bowl ever got as high as the feeling of anticipation."

Kansas point guard Kirk Hinrich

"I think the part I really enjoy is during a game there's going to be adversity, everything's not going to go right, and to come through and come out on top is the best feeling. If you're playing a good team and get down early and come back to win—that's what I personally enjoy the most. That's a thrill."

Illinois forward Lucas Johnson

"How can you not love a sport like basketball? It offers so many things that a true competitor is looking for. The feel that one gets when there is little time on the clock and the ball is in your hands. The feeling that one gets when your team loses by one on a heartbreaking buzzer-beater. The feeling one gets when you lose yourself in the moment and are so elated for your teammates that you don't care that you have been sitting at the end of the bench all game. The highs, the lows, the good and the bad—that's what makes basketball so unbelievable.

"The realization that you are playing a true team sport. The idea that every piece of the puzzle is important and that everyone wins together and loses together. The camaraderie that takes place between the participants, knowing that we are the luckiest people on earth to be able to play a game that we love so much."

Orlando Magic point guard Darrell Armstrong

"The things that the players do on the floor: Not knowing how you're going to get a defensive stop, and you end up getting it. Those are the things that makes a player feel good. Especially when you play against a player like Allen Iverson. He's so quick and can score in so many ways. You don't know which way he's going to go."

Former NHL defenseman Ray Bourque

"Asking to be traded to Colorado two years ago after spending the first 20-plus seasons of my career in Boston was the hardest thing in my life. But I still thought I could contribute and I wanted a chance to not have to quit as the player in the NHL who has played the longest without a Stanley Cup. As if it isn't enough to have passion just to play the game at 40, I knew I'd have to do more. I knew I'd have to be in the best shape of my life coming to training camp (that final year)."

Anaheim Mighty Ducks left winger Paul Kariya

"You never stop learning in this sport. And you never know

where you're going to find a tip that's going to help your game. I remember about four years ago I was rummaging through an old book and video store in Dallas and I came upon this video of Brett Hull, showing you how to shoot and smile more.

"Some people may think I'm nuts, but if you are going to be the best you can be, you have to pay attention to details. I remember going to the World Tournament one year and they put me on a line with Brendan Shanahan. I went up to him and introduced myself and asked him if he still liked to one-time drop passes near the top of the left face-off circle and if he had changed his preference on wanting passes just ahead of him at either side of the net. He looked at me like I was a spy or alien or something because I knew so much about him."

Cincinnati Reds pitcher Chris Reitsma

"To me, there's also something about the continual chase for perfection. You know you can't achieve it, but it makes you want to keep coming back for more."

New York Mets pitcher Al Leiter

"What I think is so special about our game is it is based on failure. The greatest hitters in our game fail seven out of 10 times. Because of this insecurity, because of the fact that its based on the failure that lies around the corner, it also is what makes this so exciting as a player. Because of the anxiety and the euphoric feeling you feel when you set out to do something, and you accomplish it."

Cincinnati Bengals linebacker Takeo Spikes

"Being able to go out early in the week and seeing that not only does (a plan) work in practice, but making it work in a game. That's a big satisfaction.

"As much as it hurts (never playing in a playoff game), I want it to hurt so I can come back in and push everybody. I want it to hurt. The truth hurts and the truth is: We didn't do what it took to get our asses out on that field in January. It's hard looking into the mirror and telling yourself, 'I cheated today.' It's hard. You can come up with every excuse in the world why you didn't do this and didn't do that.

"That's why I try to confront myself. Other people are going to confront you, but to put yourself on front street. That's your own motivator. That's your drive. That's the reason why you have success—because you are your best critic."

CHAPTER 9

Eyes for Another

Eyes for Another

The competitive spirit is a glowing ember inside of every athlete, just waiting for a dash of fuel and a breath of oxygen to burn brightly again. Baseball or jacks. Basketball or H-O-R-S-E. Hockey or hide-and-go-seek. Any game serves to fan the flames.

Those playing at the highest levels of a sport are no different. Some excel in one particular sport, while maintaining a love for another game, or games. Success has carried them in one athletic direction, but they never lose their passion for another game.

Eyes for Another

San Diego Chargers quarterback Doug Flutie

"I've always enjoyed playing basketball more than football. Football just kind of picked me. When I look at baseball players, many of them don't look too tired. If I played baseball, not that it's an easy game—it isn't—I could play until I'm 50. I was an above-average baseball player. I'd find a way to get on base. But I love to play basketball and use my quickness. I'm not a great shooter. I'm an assist guy. I love to see the floor."

Washington Wizards shooting guard Richard Hamilton

"I love football. It was another thing that was competitive. All of my friends, we'd play basketball in the summer time and football in the winter. Until I got to a certain stage in my life where I said, 'Football is not me because I don't like the physical contact.' But that's when I just stuck with basketball. I played wide receiver and a lot of that comes from running across the middle and letting guys hit you when you're not expecting it."

New York Jets free safety Damien Robinson

"I'd be in the NBA (half-jokingly). I averaged 17 points per game in high school and got recruited by a lot of D-1 colleges— UNLV, all the Southwest Conference schools, Long Beach, Nebraska. Kurt Thomas was my center (at Hillcrest High School). I love playing basketball, and I do it a lot in the offseason.

"But with basketball, you really need a great game. Ain't but five players on the court. There are so many schools. That's what I looked at. You have to stick out, and I wasn't a 6-5 shooting guard. At my size, going up against Allen Iverson, Gary Payton, Jason Kidd, you better have a real serious game.

"As a point guard, which is what I played, you could take control of the game. Playing defense in football, you have to wait for something to happen in order to make a play. In basketball, you have to make a play every time. It'll show up if you're not producing. You can get exposed very easily."

Former Minnesota Twins coach and baseball player Paul Molitor

"I only played hockey when I was young, but I always thought that playing hockey on the professional level would be very intense, and the fact that you're kind of putting on skates and going onto an enclosed area.

"There's something about watching a professional hockey game in person, especially at playoff time, that really has an energy that to me is pretty special. I was a lot better basketball player than hockey player, but to me playing professional hockey would have been pretty cool."

Oakland Raiders team executive and Pro Football Hall of Famer Jim Otto

"I played hockey, and if I hadn't been in football I'd have been a professional hockey player. I loved the fast action and the contact. Once again, I was tough and I wanted to be a tough guy and I love tough things. In high school and little bit after that I played a little bit of semipro hockey, I played goalie. I didn't wear a mask or I didn't wear anything like that or headgear. I was in the cage and anybody came in my crease it was war. I didn't mind the contact that I took from wing men and centers coming down on me. I loved to hit 'em. I would have loved to play hockey."

Pittsburgh Pirates infielder Pokey Reese

"Football. I just love getting out there knowing that you're going to beat somebody. I loved being a receiver. That's what I played as a freshman and sophomore and junior. They made me play quarterback as a senior. I loved going deep. I loved going across the middle, running hitches, juking a guy and going 80 yards."

Former Oklahoma linebacker Rocky Calmus

"I played basketball and baseball. I had elbow trouble and had to give up baseball. I love basketball. I like college better. It's competitive. You are playing for a school, not for more money or

a bigger contract. They are more passionate. I had to stop playing.
It was too rough on my body, all the bouncing up and down. If I
was quicker and could shoot, or if I was taller and could dunk, I
think I would play that game."

Tennessee Titans offensive lineman Brad Hopkins

"Basketball, definitely, that was my first passion. It's the flair.
It's the excitement of the game. It's actually playing offense and
defense and you can take control and be a pivotal point of that
game. There are some football players that can do that, running
backs and defensive ends who can really take control of a game
and affect the outcome. But in basketball all five members on the
floor have the chance to do just that. That kind of excitement. The
crowds aren't as big as football, but that kind of excitement and
flamboyancy and flair really adds something to that competition
level."

Texas forward Chris Owens

"I wish I could really get into mountain climbing. I'm not sure
if that's a sport or not, but that's something that I'd really like to

do. I just went to an IMAX theater and saw a movie on mountain climbers and amazing caves. Man, that is one of the most intense, extreme type of things you could ever do. It pushes you every time since there isn't much margin for error. I love being outdoors, doing stuff on the lake and stuff like that, but I've never mountain climbed. That's something I'd like to try."

New York Jets running back Curtis Martin

"I was sitting with Bill (Parcells) at the (Felix) Trinidad fight at (Madison Square Garden), and I tapped him on the shoulder during the fight and I said, 'You know, this is really what I wanted to do.' (Laughs) He said, 'I don't think you could take the low blows.' I told him, 'I take enough of them in football.'

"I like boxing. There's something about that one-on-one challenge: I'm going to beat you, I'm going to be tougher."

NASCAR driver Elliott Sadler

"I'm sure if I wasn't racing I would have tried basketball or baseball. I'm pretty sure I could have made it in baseball, I was really good in that sport. But racing definitely came first. The knee operations I had put me behind in baseball and basketball, so now I have a sit-down job so it makes it a lot easier."

Oakland Raiders fullback Jon Ritchie

"I have a lot of respect for wrestling, like high-school wrestling, not so much pro wrestling, but Greco-Roman and Olympic wrestlers. If you've ever wrestled, that is the most demanding and physically exhausting, combative sport there is. I have more respect for those guys than you can believe. Very, very tough and very demanding."

NFL defensive end Michael McCrary

"I would play basketball, because you can be so much of a factor is a game. If it's not basketball, then it would be martial arts. I like the hand-to-hand combat, which are some of the techniques I use on the field."

New York Jets coach Herman Edwards

"It would be golf, just because of the rules—honesty, and you get to compete against yourself. It's a very mentally tough game.

It has a way of bringing your emotions out, and it has a way of controlling your emotions. That's why I like it so much."

Seattle Seahawks defensive lineman John Randle

"Baseball. That's kind of my little side secret. I like to play baseball. I played in a lot of little games and I always go to the batting cage and hit the fast balls. I always wondered, 'Man, I'd love to play it.' It's something I'm passionate about. Sports have always been a part of my life. I'm not a person that could sit behind a desk all day. I've got to be outside, be moving around, sweating. I guess that's why one of my hobbies is working in my yard. I like to get sweaty and dirty, and I love that. Put my headphones on and I'm set for the day."

Pittsburgh Steelers strong safety Lee Flowers

"I went to school with a couple of great baseball players at Georgia Tech, with Jason Varitek and Nomar Garciaparra. Those guys, every time I see them play it's just a thrill to me to see those guys because I wonder some times if I ever kept up with the sport could I be in a Boston uniform or a Baltimore uniform or for that matter a Pittsburgh uniform.

"It's definitely baseball, that's one sport you can play and don't reach your prime until you're 35. You can play that sport forever. If I had to do it all over again, I'd still play football because that's my nature and that's my heart, but at the same time I wouldn't mind being a player like Bo Jackson or Deion Sanders for that matter."

CBS broadcaster and former NFL player Craig James

"As much as I love football, baseball is 1A. I was a fairly decent baseball player, then when my brother went on to play 10 years of pro baseball, I followed it. I still read the box scores daily. There is something about baseball, when you go to a game, and you are sitting in the stands, and you are watching the infield movement, and you are watching the coaches, and you're watching the way plays develop, it too is a wonderful sport. The strategy in baseball, if you really follow the game, is awesome. It's an individual sport, yet a team sport."

Philadelphia Flyers right winger Rick Tocchet

"I love football. Sometimes it's nice to hit a guy like a quarterback when he doesn't even expect. In hockey most of the time, the guys are expecting or they are hitting you, so it's nice to hit somebody else."

CHAPTER 10

Does It Matter

Does It Matter

Talent alone is not enough. The people making personnel decisions with most sports teams are looking for that special athlete who is both physically blessed and emotionally obsessed. They want somebody who skipped out of piano lessons as a kid just to throw around a ball or play street hockey. They want somebody with passion for their game.

But how do they recognize it? They can't measure passion with a JUGS radar gun, or a stopwatch. Companies providing sports data don't keep passion stats like earned-run averages or yards after the catch. NFL draft prospects take a Wonderlic test for intelligence, which is strictly a matter for the brain. Desire comes from the soul, grows in the heart and engulfs the mind.

There is no litmus test for passion, but if there was such a thing, we know who would pay for the results.

Does It Matter

Atlanta Hawks general manager Pete Babcock

"It's extremely important that you have assembled players on your roster who have a great passion for what you do. All teams try to find, devise ways where they can measure that through interviews, through observations, scouting and background checks on players. You try to find out as much as you can about a player's background and how hard he works at the game and how much he loves the game, because you certainly have a better chance at success if you have a great passion for it.

"I'd venture to say that if you talk to all 29 teams in the NBA, they would all have some similar tests and some different tests. In terms

of written tests that we give, we give two different tests and one

of them is specifically designed, it's like an athletic inventory, to

try to measure those types of things: competitiveness, mental

toughness and love for the game, and those kinds of things. None

of these things is foolproof, but it's just another tool you use.

"Our staff will be on the phones constantly talking to people,

asking questions specifically about: Does this player love to play?

Does he have a great passion for the game? Does he want to be

good?

"Our view will be that an individual who has a burning desire

to be successful and wants to be as good as he possibly can be at

anything, this translates into them being a pretty effective player,

given the assumption that they are talented.

"We try to take everything. We look at them as pieces of a

puzzle, and try not to make a decision based on just one piece,

but collectively put it all together and see how it plays out. We've

found over the years that the individual pieces are sometimes

wrong. It may be the written test that gives you a false read. It may

be just the interview by itself that gives you a false read. But, if you put it all together it usually paints a fairly accurate picture."

San Diego Padres general manager Kevin Towers

"The day-in and day-out grind. Where at least in the NFL, you're playing 16 weekends, but to go out and play every single night you have to have a passion for the game or you'll run into burnout real soon.

"I don't think you every truly know until you're around a player and you see how he prepares himself. The perfect example we got is a guy like Trevor Hoffman, who is always the last guy out of the clubhouse. You don't see that often any more. This guy is a closer and the preparation that he puts into his game. He's one of those guys that doesn't want to take his uniform off. That uniform means so much to him and he realized how hard he has to work to wear that uniform. I think he really appreciates where he's at right now and he's got a tremendous passion for it and hates to take the uniform off.

"A lot of times I'll have meetings with our manager and I'll be leaving the clubhouse after midnight and there's Hoffy still sitting there with his uniform on.

"You can always tell guys who have passion for the game because even in their down time they're watching video or watching a major league game on TV. They want to be around the game 24-7, or talk about the game.

"Look at Rickey Henderson. To be 42 years of age and playing the game with the intensity that he still has, you have to have passion.

"These guys would love to sit around and talk baseball to you.

"We used to sit in spring training and he'd say, you know, this uniform means too much to me.

"I happened to go our fantasy camp this year in the offseason. We had it out in Peoria (Ariz.). Randy Jones was there, Nate Colbert, Norm Sherry and Bruce Bochy. To hear these guys talking to the campers and talking about how that fantasy camp to them was probably more enjoyable then to the actual campers. Just because of putting the uniform back on. How much it meant to them, even though they are 40 or 50 years old, getting to put a major league baseball uniform back on and what that felt like and bringing back memories of how much it meant to them.

"It's amazing. You have to have passion to even go back and

do that. I imagine it happens in other fantasy camps, but to sit there and listen to former major league players who have had great careers sit there with 50 campers and say, 'As much fun as you've had, we've had a better time.' Just competing again and putting the uniform on again.

"We have somebody who works for our ballclub that during the amateur draft interviews all the potential draftees. I would imagine that's part of it, psych evaluation, plus asking particular questions to a would-be player you start to find out how much the game means to that player."

New York Giants general manager Ernie Accorsi

"I think it does make a difference. It's ironic that you would ask that because a year ago during the offseason we were coming off a 7-9 season and Jim (Fassel) and I did not like the chemistry in the locker room. And Jim said to me, 'We've got to find players who love playing football. We have guys around here who don't love playing football.' I think that is something that we really found when we picked up Glenn Parker and Lomas Brown and those kind of guys is they love the game.

"If you don't love it, it's too hard to play it for money. I don't care how much money it is. It's too tough a game. We are always looking for people who play the game with a joy. How do you define that? You have to trust your instincts in defining it. You try to get to know the player before you acquire him. Or you study the way he plays. You usually can tell if he plays with a joy and love of the game. To me, I don't think you can win without it.

"I think more than anything else. We all have these systems and forms, check points, strong points, weak points, critical factors. I think they're all important, you have to have a structure and some sort of discipline to your scouting. But in the final analysis, when you try to determine that quality, you feel it in your stomach. That, you just have to trust your instincts on.

"When a big game is decided or a championship is on the line, the game is going to go to the person who loves the game more than the person who doesn't. I just believe that. And you have to somehow see it with your eyes and your stomach. It's not something that you're going to be able to figure out with your ears, by what somebody tells you, or with your pencil and your charts.

"The Steelers who won four (Super Bowls) in six years—from

Bradshaw to Swann, from Lambert to Mean Joe Greene—they played with an ebullience. You could see they loved playing. They were not a faceless machine-like team. They played with emotion. They just played with a joy that you can see with a lot of championship teams. Sure, they're going to take the money and it's a great way to make a living. Players like that who make a difference and love playing the game, if they were making what they made in 1955, they'd still play, because they love the game.

"We have testing. I don't discount any ingredient to the evaluation of a player. But I really think to determine it, in the final analysis, you got to feel it.

"It's a difference-maker in our position. I don't care how much money they make, they play for the love of the game. They really do. You can see it. There are guys out there who you can see don't, and you don't want those guys around.

"You have to feel, when you walk out on that field on Sunday, you have to feel like there's nowhere on earth I'd rather be than here today. This is where I want to be. If you have that, that's what makes it so tough to walk away from, for all of them."

CHAPTER 11

Hall of Fame

Hall of Fame

Some people are good at what they do. Others are great.

Then there are those who are respected by the others in their field, both good and great, not so much because of achievement, but more so for their fervor.

Those who play sports at the highest levels often ooze an excess of self confidence. However, they are not beyond recognizing an individual with an intense desire and passion for the game that exceeds and inspires others in their game.

Hall of Fame

Oakland Raiders team executive and Pro Football Hall of Famer Jim Otto

"When I see a player that somehow emulates me—a guy who is doing the same thing that I did or that I would do the same thing he's doing—it kind of tickles me and I enjoy that. When I see an extra effort or when I see a great block by somebody or a great play, it can be a wide receiver catching a tremendous pass. I wasn't a receiver but that's the way I would have wanted to catch it and you know it makes me feel good."

Houston Rockets point guard Steve Francis

"I really think Kevin Garnett has a lot of passion for the game. Sometimes people talk about him because he is always talking, but he loves playing basketball and nobody can ever take his passion away. They can take his money away from him, but they can never take his passion because he is always going to love the game."

Washington Wizards shooting guard Richard Hamilton

"Michael Jordan and Magic Johnson, them guys that really had that passion for the game because early in Michael's career he wasn't winning and there was a whole lot of doubt about his game and people were saying he could never carry his team to a championship. And with that passion and everything he did, he proved everybody wrong and won not just one but many championships."

NFL defensive back Blaine Bishop

"Hands down, it's Ronnie Lott. When I was growing up I loved Ronnie Lott and Walter Payton. Those guys played the game with a passion that I don't think anybody else had, that work ethic. I used to read articles about them, they strived to be better than the best. There was something inside of them that pushed them beyond limits, and it showed up in games. Their energy level to be the best and make their team the best was just on a whole other level. I think they made a difference in every game."

Former NBA player Austin Carr

"I grew up watching Dave Bing and Elgin Baylor. Those were guys that were right before me that I grew up watching. They controlled the game and did a little bit of everything. That used to be fascinating to me, to have one guy that could do pretty much everything. I wanted to be like that."

U.S. Congressman and former college football player J.C. Watts

"I usually find myself homing in on the quarterbacks. The one that comes to mind that I always was fascinated with is Joe Montana. God, his knack and his passion to find a way to win. Joe didn't look physically like or have the physical stature of John Elway or Warren Moon, but he obviously understood that Al Davis motto of 'Just win, baby.' He did it very well. And then you take a John Elway, who just had the physical tools of mobility, strong arm and a great mind and just willed himself to win both physically and mentally. I kind of like Brett Favre. Brett's a brawler. He kind of reminds me of a middle linebacker that's playing quarterback. You love to watch him because I've often said to my friends he's a street fighter playing quarterback. Warren (Moon) was just plum good, physically and mentally. When he was 40 he was still throwing the ball with the best of them.

"Those guys, I've always appreciated the contribution they've made to the game and I've always appreciated their passion for it. To just go out, year in and year out and compete. That silliness of guys saying, 'I love this game so much I'd do it for free.' I don't believe that. I do think those guys, when they played, there was a passion and a love for what they were doing that you could see it in their performance. They encourage you, as you are sitting on your couch watching the football game on Sunday afternoon, watching those guys play tends to muster up the competitive juices again."

Connecticut basketball coach Jim Calhoun

"I think there's been a lot of different people (who represent passion for basketball for me). I think probably the most up-close and personal guy, because I was around Boston all those years, was Dave Cowens, at 6-foot-8, being an All-Star center. I thought the passion with which Larry Bird made himself into such a great player was phenomenal. When I think of passion in Boston I would think really of those two guys. Two self-made players who just did phenomenal things with what they had.

"And I watch a Larry Brown—Larry's what, 61 now I think—and I watch him still after zillions of games agonize over a turnover or a blown defensive assignment. That's passion. That's passion. It's nice to see, too, because I have people that say to me, 'Well, you don't have to (be passionate). You've won a national championship, and you've won this many.' No, it's that you really do have to, in ways, be passionate because that's what you are. Some guys don't show their passion. I happen to do that, and that's hopefully what makes me successful."

NASCAR crew chief Shawn Parker

"(Mark Martin) didn't do it because he had to, he did because he wants to. He loves to race and it shows what type of driver he is and he wants to win. Whatever it takes, he will do it whether he is in a cast or crippled up or whatever. It's what he's grown up with.

"I've heard them tell stories of when Mark was in ASA (American Speed Association) when he had broken feet and arms. He just has determination. An injury is supposed to slow you down, but if you put your mind to it, nothing should slow you down. That's what Mark has proven, and that's just the kind of driver he is."

Pittsburgh Steelers strong safety Lee Flowers

"Walter Payton. I can remember the commercial, I want to say it was a KangaRoos commercial, I'm not sure. Every time I think about my workout regimen, I think about Payton (in that commercial) just running up this huge mountain. He kept doing it over and over and over until he couldn't walk no more. You could just tell by the way he ran on the field, he always ran like he was trying to overcome a mountain. Most guys will say Walter Payton because his work habits were just unreal. He was probably the only running back, beside Earl Campbell, looking to hit you before you hit him."

Indianapolis Colts quarterback Peyton Manning

"I had a chance to be around Junior Seau a couple times. I think Junior is somewhat of a throwback, when he plays, he doesn't hold anything back and I've played against him about three times. He is truly playing with a passion inside him. Junior has an appreciation for the former great linebackers and for the former great players who have played in the NFL. To have a true passion, you have to love everything about the game, going off today and what's happened in the past."

Pro Football Hall of Famer Jack Ham

"I played against a guy named Roger Staubach, who I saw taking shots, especially from our defensive line during the Super Bowl, and we thought we had control of the game, and this guy ended up making it a little closer for all of us—maybe he took a couple years off my life. I never saw a guy with the toughness in the quarterback position like that and take all those shots and just his will in trying to bring his team back, I'll always have great admiration for Staubach."

Detroit Lions CEO and president and former NFL player and broadcaster Matt Millen

"John Madden loves football. I've had two real major football influences for football in my life. One is my high-school coach (in Whitehall, Pa.) Andy Melosky, who loves football as much as anybody, and the other is Madden, who could draw the same parallels from all of his respective businesses—and there are a bunch—and he could apply those things that he took from football. John just loves it, because John knows it's bigger than just a game."

Former NFL player Andy Russell

"This is a classic passion-for-the-game story. Ernie Stautner comes in the huddle and his thumb is broken back against his wrist. There's a tear near the break, and his bone is sticking out. He has a compound fracture of the thumb. He takes his thumb in his hand and he wrenches it down into his fist. Doesn't show it to anybody. Doesn't say anything. Looks up and says, 'What's the defense?' And I thought to myself, 'I'm not in the right business.

This guy has a compound fracture of the thumb, and he's not even going to leave the game.'

"So he stayed there for the rest of that series, and then we came off, and I'm watching him because I'm the only guy who saw that he had a compound fracture. I saw the bone. So I'm figuring now he's going to ask for the doctor and he may have to go to the hospital because this thing could get infected, and he says, 'Give me some tape.' So they throw him some tape and he just starts taping this huge ball. He makes this big fist. Then we go back in. He plays the entire game. Never misses a down. I'm just astounded, and he's using this hand which is broken as a club. He's beating people with it. After the game, we go into the locker room and he says, 'Hey Doc, I think I got a problem.' And I'm thinking this is just unbelievable. That is passion for what you do. That guy was making no money. He just loved to play. What a commitment."

"The classic is Rocky Bleier. Rocky Bleier is the only player to go to Vietnam and be wounded in combat and come back and play in the NFL. When he came back, he had a bullet wound in his thigh and shrapnel in his foot, and he was about 178 pounds.

The Rooneys were very nice to him. ... but no one expected him to really play again. He got a call from Chuck Knoll in the offseason saying, 'Rocky, you should really not come back to camp. You should—as Knoll used to say—'Seek your life's work.' Instead of doing that, Rocky chose to hire a physical trainer. When he was a rookie before he went to Vietnam, he was 5-8, 185 pounds and ran a 4.8 40. He made the team on guts and effort. Just that kind of a guy. He came back after Vietnam decimated by the wound, but then he built himself up to 230 through weightlifting, and he ran a 4.5. And he worked himself up to the starting halfback position where, essentially, he was primarily a blocker for Franco Harris. Franco moved the ball well when Rocky was in there, but in 1976, (Bleier) had a 1,000-yard rushing year. That's a phenomenal story. That is a story of passion because if the head coach calls you and tells you you ought to give it up, and you drop everything and just become a fanatical conditioning guy, (you've got to have passion)."

Tampa Bay Buccaneers safety John Lynch

"Hardy Nickerson. He loves the game of football. That's what

cracks me up, when people talk about how players play for the
money. Well, yeah, they do to a certain extent, but you can't fool
people. They can tell your true colors. Hardy had a total commitment to the game, in-season and out-of-season. He showed that
by taking notes in team meetings and being a professional. Hardy
was a fairly reserved guy like me—I'm a fairly reserved guy—but
he had another personality on the field. You get into the competition and something happens. You're wild and crazy. You lose
your inhibitions. That's not a conscious thing. It just happens.
You're out there, and you're competing. That's one thing, if you've
talked to guys who have played for a long time and have retired,
they know that the passion is not there anymore. If you're a player who's played with passion, it's hard."

St. Louis Rams wide receiver Torry Holt

"I feel there are still a lot of athletes out there with the old
soul who really love the game like the Jim Browns and the
Walter Paytons. Those guys really loved the game. They would
play with bloody knuckles. The Jack Youngbloods and the Jack
Lamberts, who would be knocked out and they'd still be out

there barking calls, because they loved and had a passion for playing football. Those guys set the tempo for us."

Pro Football Hall of Famer Steve Largent

"Walter Payton to me was a guy I think of. I saw him play for the Bears when they were 1-15, and I saw him play for the Bears when they were 15-1, and the guy played at the same speed and the same intensity and the same enthusiasm regardless of what the team's record was for the season. I remember (Seahawks safety) Kenny Easley saying that Walter Payton would hit you as hard as you hit him. He would always bounce up with a smile on his face and a bounce in his step. He played hard, win or lose. When I think about a guy who really played the game the way I think it should have been played on every play, I think of Payton. Well, he was such a class guy. Some guys you get the sense that they have to hate you in order to perform well and to get the intensity level that they need to have, but not Payton. There was never a time that I'd see Walter, on the field or off the field, that he wouldn't come up and greet me with a hug. He loved football, he loved life and he loved people. I think he just personified everything that's great about sports and everything that's great about football."